THE
Canadian Living
20TH ANNIVERSARY
COOKBOOK

CONTENTS

INTRODUCTION

CANADIAN LIVING is a privileged guest in millions of Canadian homes. We appreciate this ongoing invitation to share home-cooked food at the table with our readers whatever the occasion — on busy weeknights, when company comes for family get-togethers or at joyous celebrations such as showers, weddings and birthdays.

From the very beginning, 20 years ago, our founding food editor, Carol Ferguson, set a standard of excellence for home cooking in Canada. "My aim was to introduce readers to the kinds of dishes they had heard about and wanted to make at home, such as the quiches and crêpes that were so popular then," says Ferguson. "I also set out to test and retest for the perfect versions of our most popular and enduring Canadian dishes — tourtière, lemon meringue pie, chocolate chip cookies and split pea soup are some examples."

Cajun Fish Kabobs, page 90

Quick Skillet Lasagna, page 12

These standards of great home cooking remain the goal of *Canadian Living*, although the choice of dishes exciting Canadians these days has shifted to the likes of *Thai Beef Salad* and *Chicken Tortilla Soup*. As well, we continue to perfect new classics such as *Sesame Seed Bagels* and *Grilled Vegetable Pizza*, dishes reflecting the adventuresome tastebuds and the varied cooking backgrounds of Canadians today.

As *Canadian Living* became more successful, the magazine expanded and was enriched by regular special food editions. Carol Ferguson was joined by other food writers, now major figures in Canada — Margaret Fraser, Anne Lindsay, Rose Murray, Iris Raven, Kay Spicer and Bonnie Stern. In 1987, when Carol Ferguson left to head up *Canadian Living's Food*, I took up the post as

Bean Soup with Carrot Salsa, page 28

food editor of *Canadian Living*. Our model test kitchen had been up and running for a number of years, first under the direction of Beth Moffatt, then Patricia Jamieson and now Daphna Rabinovitch. Our Tested till Perfect motto, which grew out of a meticulous method of testing and retesting as often as necessary, provides that reassuring guarantee to our readers that if it is a *Canadian Living* recipe, you can be confident that it will not only work but that it will please you and the people who sit down with you.

Canadian Living works to simplify cooking, cutting out unnecessary steps and cleanup. Together with contributing nutrition editor Anne Lindsay, we look to Canada's Food Guide to Healthy Eating, trimming fats and encouraging the use of grains, nutritious

Savory Herb Cheesecake, page 114

vegetables and fruits, lower-fat dairy products and lean, sensible portions of meat, poultry, fish and meat alternatives. Of course, some entertaining and festive-occasion dishes, notably desserts, may not fall as easily into these guidelines; we recommend that readers balance their meals to accommodate these sweet pleasures.

Deep-Dish Peach Crisp, page 162

Now, as 20 years ago, *Canadian Living* focuses on great home cooking. Planning and preparing meals, then sharing them together, are important pleasures in life. Through them, traditions are passed on. Thank you for sharing our table.

Elizabeth Baird
Food Director
Canadian Living magazine

ACKNOWLEDGMENTS

HATS OFF TO EVERYONE who has been part of the creation of this beautiful commemorative cookbook: associate publisher Caren King, who took up the challenge of packaging the book, our enthusiastic publisher, Greg MacNeil, editor-in-chief Bonnie Baker Cowan, project editor Carol Sherman, designer Andrew Smith, and right-hand people Beverley Renahan, Daphna Rabinovitch and all the members of the test kitchen team — Donna Bartolini, Kate Gammal, Heather Howe, Jennifer MacKenzie and Dana McCauley. A vote of thanks also goes to Julia Armstrong, Laura Bickle, Olga Goncalves, Marianne Graham, Lidija Loik, Teresa Sousa and senior editor Donna Paris.

Canadian Living's art department, formerly under Deborah Fadden and now headed by Martha Weaver, created the good-looking photography in conjunction with Canada's finest food photographers, including Fred Bird, Doug Bradshaw, Christopher Campbell, Frank Grant, Pat Lacroix, Michael Mahovlich, Michael Waring and Robert Wigington, and talented food stylists, among whom Debbi Charendoff Moses, Ruth Gangbar, Jennifer McLagan, Claire Stancer, Rosemarie Superville and Olga Truchan were principals. The task of providing the props for the shots was shared by Susan Doherty-Hannaford, Paola Giavedoni, Maggi Jones and Janet Walkinshaw. Thank you to Don Watt of The Watt Group for permission to use the detail photography.

Special thanks go to founding food editor Carol Ferguson, her associate Margaret Fraser, former test kitchen manager Patricia Jamieson and food writers Rose Murray, Iris Raven, Kay Spicer and Bonnie Stern, who have been part of *Canadian Living* throughout the 20 years that *Canadian Living* has been part of living in Canada.

NUTRIENT INFORMATION

To meet nutrient needs, a moderately active woman 20 to 50 years old needs about 1,900 calories, 45 g protein, 60 g fat and 250 g carbohydrate daily. Men and teenagers usually need more.

The analysis was carried out using imperial measures except when the practical recipe quantity was metric. Calculations were based on the first ingredient listed when there was a choice and did not include optional ingredients. The recipes were analysed using 2% milk.

Nutrient values have been rounded to the nearest whole number and calories to the nearest five. Following criteria outlined in the *Guide for Food Manufacturers and Advertisers, Revised Edition 1988* (Consumer and Corporate Affairs, Canada), recipes have been identified that are excellent or good sources of iron or calcium, and/or contain high or very high amounts of dietary fibre.

Nutrient analysis of the recipes was performed by Beverley Bell-Rowbotham and Barbara Selley of Info Access (1988) Inc. using the nutritional accounting component of the CBORD Menu Management System. The nutrient database was the 1991 Canadian Nutrient File, supplemented when necessary with documented data from reliable sources.

CHAPTER ONE

FAST TRACK SUPPERS

Some rush hours are on the road, but others, just as real, are in the kitchen. Chances are it's a weeknight and the time squeeze is between arriving home from school and work and getting out the door to practices, lessons and meetings. Here's culinary inspiration for those evenings.

Grilled Vegetable Pizza

Summer can last all year when you top pizza with grilled vegetables. In barbecue season, grill extra vegetables one day for pizza the next night. When it's too cold, use an indoor grill or broiler for crisp-edged veggies.

1	small eggplant	1
1	zucchini	1
2 tbsp	olive oil	25 mL
1	12-inch (30 cm) prebaked pizza crust	1
¼ cup	pesto	50 mL
1 tbsp	chopped fresh oregano (or 1 tsp/5 mL dried)	15 mL
¼ cup	sliced red onion	50 mL
1 cup	shredded part-skim mozzarella cheese	250 mL

- Slice eggplant crosswise and zucchini lengthwise into ¼-inch (5 mm) thick slices; brush with oil. Place on greased grill over medium-high heat; cover and cook, turning once, for about 5 minutes or until well marked and tender.

- Place pizza crust on pizza pan or baking sheet; spread with pesto. Cover with grilled eggplant and zucchini; sprinkle with oregano. Arrange red onion over top; sprinkle with cheese.

- Bake in 500°F (260°C) oven for 8 to 10 minutes, or on covered greased grill for about 12 minutes, or until crust is crisp and cheese is melted and bubbly.

Makes 1 pizza, or 4 pieces.
PER PIECE: about 420 calories, 15 g protein, 21 g fat, 43 g carbohydrate, high source fibre, excellent source calcium, good source iron.

TIP: Pesto is readily available in the supermarket, but you can just as easily make your own: In food processor, finely chop 1 cup (250 mL) packed fresh basil, ½ cup (125 mL) freshly grated Parmesan cheese, 2 tbsp (25 mL) pine nuts, 1 large clove garlic and ½ tsp (2 mL) each salt and pepper. With motor running, gradually pour in ½ cup (125 mL) olive oil, processing until smooth. Makes about 1 cup (250 mL).

Herb-Grilled Pizza with Prosciutto

Kneading herbs into pizza dough and sprinkling them over a cheesy, crispy-thin crust lets you celebrate herbs at their finest.

¼ cup	chopped fresh parsley	50 mL
2 tbsp	chopped fresh oregano	25 mL
1 lb	pizza dough	500 g
	Cornmeal	
2 tbsp	olive oil	25 mL
2½ cups	shredded Fontina cheese (½ lb/250 g)	625 mL
⅔ cup	tomato sauce	150 mL
¼ cup	chopped fresh basil	50 mL
6	thin slices prosciutto or ham, coarsely chopped	6

- On lightly floured surface, knead parsley and oregano into dough until evenly distributed. Cut in half and form into balls; cover and let rest for 15 minutes. Roll out each ball thinly to make 12-inch (30 cm) round.

- Place each pizza round on cornmeal-dusted pizza pan; brush with some of the oil. Scatter cheese evenly over top; spoon tomato sauce over cheese. Drizzle with remaining oil.

- Place in 500°F (260°C) oven or on covered greased grill over medium-high heat; cook for about 12 minutes or until crust is crisp and cheese is melted and bubbly. Scatter basil and prosciutto over top.

Makes 4 servings.
PER SERVING: about 630 calories, 27 g protein, 31 g fat, 59 g carbohydrate, excellent source calcium and iron.

Quick Skillet Lasagna

Ham adds its succulence to a quick tomato sauce that's chunky with vegetables. Mix it with pasta and top it with ricotta and mozzarella for a lasagna with a friendly Italian taste.

4 cups	rotini pasta	1 L
1 tsp	vegetable oil	5 mL
2	zucchini, cubed	2
1	onion, chopped	1
Half	sweet red or green pepper, diced	Half
4 cups	sliced mushrooms (¾ lb/375 g)	1 L
1½ cups	diced cooked ham	375 mL
1 tsp	dried oregano	5 mL
¼ tsp	pepper	1 mL
1	jar (375 mL) spaghetti sauce	1
1	tub (475 g) light ricotta cheese	1
2 cups	shredded part-skim mozzarella cheese	500 mL

- In pot of boiling salted water, cook rotini until tender but firm, about 6 minutes. Drain in colander; set aside.

- Meanwhile, in nonstick ovenproof skillet, heat oil over medium-high heat; cook zucchini, onion, red pepper, mushrooms, ham, oregano and pepper for 8 minutes or until tender, tossing often.

- Add spaghetti sauce; cook, stirring occasionally, for 5 minutes. Stir in pasta. Spread ricotta evenly over top; sprinkle with mozzarella. Broil for 5 minutes or until golden brown.

Makes 6 servings.
PER SERVING: about 565 calories, 36 g protein, 18 g fat, 64 g carbohydrate, high source fibre, excellent source calcium, good source iron.

Fusilli with Creamy Tomato Herb Sauce

When it comes to convenience, you can't beat herbed cream cheese. It adds a variety of herbs and guarantees a thick, creamy sauce without the fuss of reducing whipping cream.

1 tbsp	olive oil	15 mL
1	onion, chopped	1
1	can (28 oz/796 mL) tomatoes, puréed	1
¼ tsp	pepper	1 mL
1	pkg (113 g) herbed cream cheese	1
4 cups	fusilli pasta	1 L
¼ cup	freshly grated Parmesan cheese	50 mL
1 tbsp	chopped fresh parsley	15 mL

- In skillet, heat oil over medium heat; cook onion, stirring occasionally, for 3 minutes or until softened.

- Add tomatoes and pepper; bring to boil. Reduce heat and simmer for 10 to 12 minutes or until thickened. Whisk in cream cheese until smooth and bubbly.

- Meanwhile, in large saucepan of boiling salted water, cook fusilli for 8 to 10 minutes or until tender but firm. Drain and toss with sauce. Sprinkle with Parmesan and parsley.

Makes 4 servings.
PER SERVING: about 525 calories, 18 g protein, 17 g fat, 75 g carbohydrate, very high source fibre, good source calcium and iron.

The Ultimate in Spaghetti Sauces

You can simmer these fresh-tasting sauces in no time to top any pasta. Freeze half if that suits your household numbers or create your own signature sauces with additions such as mushrooms, fennel and Italian sausage.

LIGHT AND HERBY BASIC SAUCE

2 tsp	olive oil	10 mL
3	cloves garlic, minced	3
2	onions, chopped	2
1	carrot, grated	1
2 tsp	dried basil	10 mL
1 tsp	dried oregano	5 mL
½ tsp	salt	2 mL
¼ tsp	pepper	1 mL
2	cans (each 28 oz/796 mL) tomatoes	2
2 tbsp	tomato paste	25 mL
1 tsp	granulated sugar	5 mL
¼ cup	chopped fresh parsley	50 mL

- In large saucepan, heat oil over medium heat; cook garlic, onions, carrot, basil, oregano, salt and pepper, stirring occasionally, for 5 minutes or until softened.

- Add tomatoes, breaking up with spoon; stir in tomato paste and sugar. Bring to boil; reduce heat to medium and simmer for 40 to 45 minutes or until thickened. Stir in parsley.

Makes 6 cups (1.5 L).
PER 1 CUP (250 mL): about 100 calories, 3 g protein, 2 g fat, 19 g carbohydrate, high source fibre.

TIP: Canned tomatoes may vary in sweetness; therefore, taste and adjust sauce with about 1 tsp (5 mL) granulated sugar 5 minutes before end of cooking if necessary.

VARIATIONS

MIXED MUSHROOM SPAGHETTI SAUCE: In skillet, heat 1 tsp (5 mL) olive oil and 2 tsp (10 mL) butter over medium heat; cook 4 cups (1 L) sliced mixed fresh mushrooms (shiitake, oyster, portobello, button) for 5 to 7 minutes or until golden. Add to Light and Herby Basic Sauce along with 1 tsp (5 mL) granulated sugar; simmer for 10 minutes.

Makes 7 cups (1.75 L).
PER 1 CUP (250 mL): about 110 calories, 4 g protein, 4 g fat, 18 g carbohydrate, high source fibre.

CHUNKY VEGETABLE SPAGHETTI SAUCE: In skillet, heat 1 tbsp (15 mL) olive oil over medium heat; cook 2 cups (500 mL) cubed peeled eggplant, stirring often, for 5 minutes. Add 1 chopped sweet pepper and 1 chopped zucchini; cook for 5 minutes. Add to Light and Herby Basic Sauce along with 1 tsp (5 mL) granulated sugar; simmer for 10 minutes. Stir in 2 tbsp (25 mL) chopped fresh parsley.

Makes 8 cups (2 L).
PER 1 CUP (250 mL): about 105 calories, 3 g protein, 4 g fat, 18 g carbohydrate, high source fibre.

SAUSAGE FENNEL SPAGHETTI SAUCE: In skillet, heat 2 tsp (10 mL) olive oil over medium-high heat. Remove casings from 1 lb (500 g) mild Italian sausage; add to pan and cook for 4 minutes. Add 1 tsp (5 mL) crushed fennel seeds; cook for 1 minute. Drain off fat. Add to Light and Herby Basic Sauce; simmer for 10 minutes.

Makes 8 cups (2 L).
PER 1 CUP (250 mL): about 185 calories, 11 g protein, 10 g fat, 15 g carbohydrate.

BASIL CHICKEN OR BEEF SPAGHETTI SAUCE: In skillet, heat 2 tsp (10 mL) olive oil over medium-high heat. Add 1 lb (500 g) ground chicken or lean ground beef; cook, breaking up with spoon, for about 5 minutes or until no longer pink. Drain off any fat. Add to Light and Herby Basic Sauce; simmer for 10 minutes. Stir in ½ cup (125 mL) chopped fresh basil.

Makes 8 cups (2 L).
PER 1 CUP (250 mL): about 155 calories, 13 g protein, 5 g fat, 14 g carbohydrate.

Pastitsio Sauce

This ground beef sauce accented Greek-style with cinnamon and oregano is a delight to spoon over baked potatoes or pasta shells. Feta and walnuts round out the flavors and add a pleasing tang and crunch.

1 tbsp	vegetable oil	15 mL
1	onion, chopped	1
1	clove garlic, minced	1
1 tsp	dried oregano	5 mL
½ tsp	cinnamon	2 mL
¼ tsp	ground cumin	1 mL
1 lb	lean ground beef	500 g
1 cup	tomato sauce	250 mL
½ cup	red wine or beef stock	125 mL
⅓ cup	crumbled feta cheese	75 mL
¼ cup	toasted chopped walnuts	50 mL
2 tbsp	chopped fresh parsley	25 mL

- In large skillet, heat oil over medium heat; cook onion, garlic, oregano, cinnamon and cumin, stirring occasionally, for 4 minutes or until softened. Add beef, stirring to break up meat; cook for about 5 minutes or until no longer pink.

- Add tomato sauce and wine; bring to boil. Reduce heat, cover and simmer for about 15 minutes or until thickened.

- Spoon off any fat. Serve sprinkled with feta, walnuts and parsley.

  Makes 4 servings.
  PER SERVING: about 330 calories, 25 g protein, 21 g fat, 10 g carbohydrate, good source iron.

TIP: To toast walnuts, bake on baking sheet in 350°F (180°C) oven for about 10 minutes or until fragrant.

Solo Jambalaya

The microwave partners well with the stovetop for a creative meal for one featuring rice and sausage (preferably a zesty Italian one).

¼ lb	spicy sausage (Italian, chorizo or bratwurst)	125 g
1 tsp	vegetable oil	5 mL
2 tbsp	chopped onion	25 mL
2 tbsp	diced sweet green pepper	25 mL
⅔ cup	canned tomatoes (undrained), chopped	150 mL
¼ cup	long-grain rice	50 mL
1 tbsp	tomato paste	15 mL
¼ tsp	salt	1 mL
Pinch	each dried thyme and hot pepper flakes	Pinch

- In microwaveable pie plate, prick sausage all over with fork. Cover with waxed paper; microwave at High for 1½ minutes. Rotate and turn sausage over; microwave at High for 1 minute. (Or brown in skillet over medium-high heat.) Cut into thick slices.

- Meanwhile, in saucepan, heat oil over medium heat; cook onion and green pepper, stirring occasionally, for 2 to 3 minutes or until softened but not browned.

- Add sausage, tomatoes, rice, tomato paste, salt, thyme and hot pepper flakes; bring to boil. Cover and reduce heat; simmer gently for 20 minutes or until most of the liquid is absorbed. Let stand for 5 minutes; stir well.

  Makes 1 serving.
  PER SERVING: about 575 calories, 23 g protein, 32 g fat, 49 g carbohydrate, good source iron.

TIP: If doubling this dish, the sausage will need an extra 2 minutes or so in the microwave.

Burgers with Red Onions

Ground beef may be budget, but it has great family appeal, especially as burgers. The sweet-and-sour onions don't take much time but they add that little "sitting down with my family is important" touch.

1	egg	1
½ cup	fresh bread crumbs	125 mL
2 tbsp	tomato paste	25 mL
½ tsp	dried mint	2 mL
½ tsp	salt	2 mL
¼ tsp	pepper	1 mL
1 lb	lean ground beef	500 g
¼ cup	chopped fresh parsley	50 mL
SWEET-AND-SOUR ONIONS:		
½ tsp	vegetable oil	2 mL
1 cup	sliced red onion	250 mL
1 tbsp	liquid honey	15 mL
2 tbsp	red wine vinegar	25 mL
¼ tsp	each salt and pepper	1 mL

- In bowl, whisk egg with ¼ cup (50 mL) water, bread crumbs, tomato paste, mint, salt and pepper; mix in beef and parsley. Form into four ¾-inch (2 cm) thick patties.

- Place on greased baking sheet; broil for 5 minutes per side or until no longer pink inside.

- SWEET-AND-SOUR ONIONS: Meanwhile, in nonstick skillet, heat oil over medium-high heat; cook onion, stirring, for 2 minutes or until beginning to soften.

- Add honey, tossing to coat; cook for 1 minute. Stir in vinegar; cook for 1 minute or until onions are glossy. Season with salt and pepper. Serve with burgers.

Makes 4 servings.
PER SERVING: about 280 calories, 24 g protein, 14 g fat, 13 g carbohydrate, good source iron.

Spunky Beef Burgers

With the zip of your favorite salsa packed into these moist burgers, you might even decide to go easy on the mustard and relish. Tuck them into a bun or serve on a plate with green beans and mashed potatoes.

1	egg	1
¼ cup	dry bread crumbs	50 mL
¼ cup	salsa	50 mL
4	green onions, finely chopped	4
2	cloves garlic, minced	2
1 tbsp	Dijon mustard	15 mL
½ tsp	Worcestershire sauce	2 mL
½ tsp	salt	2 mL
¼ tsp	pepper	1 mL
Dash	hot pepper sauce	Dash
1 lb	lean ground beef	500 g
6	hamburger buns	6

- In bowl, beat egg; mix in bread crumbs, salsa, onions, garlic, mustard, Worcestershire sauce, salt, pepper and hot pepper sauce. Mix in beef; shape into six ½-inch (1 cm) thick patties.

- Place patties on greased grill over medium heat; cover and cook for about 6 minutes per side or until no longer pink inside. Sandwich in buns.

Makes 6 servings.
Per serving: about 355 calories, 21 g protein, 13 g fat, 37 g carbohydrate, good source iron.

Tip: Make the Spunky Beef Burgers up to a week ahead and freeze; allow at least 24 hours for thawing in the refrigerator. Or make them earlier in the day, cover and refrigerate for up to 8 hours. If only medium ground beef is available, don't worry; the excess fat drips off during grilling.

Chicken Patty with Rosemary for One

This burger, moist with apple and flavorful with rosemary, serves one. But, of course, it can be doubled or increased to suit the occasion.

¼ lb	ground chicken	125 g
1 tbsp	grated peeled apple	15 mL
1 tbsp	grated onion	15 mL
1 tbsp	dry bread crumbs or cracker crumbs	15 mL
½ tsp	chopped fresh rosemary (or pinch dried)	2 mL
½ tsp	prepared horseradish	2 mL
Pinch	each salt and pepper	Pinch

- In bowl, mix together chicken, apple, onion, bread crumbs, 1 tbsp (15 mL) water, rosemary, horseradish, salt and pepper.

- Shape into ½-inch (2 cm) thick patty. Broil for about 4 minutes per side or until cooked through.

Makes 1 serving.
Per serving: about 230 calories, 22 g protein, 12 g fat, 7 g carbohydrate.

PREVENTIVE PRACTICE

- Thaw meats, including poultry, in the refrigerator and not on the counter, where bacteria thrive and multiply at the higher temperature.
- Vigorously wash all dishes, utensils and cutting boards used for raw meat with soap and hot water.

- Bring a clean plate to the barbecue for cooked meats. Never put them back on plates that held uncooked meat.
- Always cook ground meats to the point where they are no longer pink inside and chicken to the point where juices run clear when the chicken is pierced.

Herbed Salmon and Asparagus Grill

Salmon grills beautifully, whether you buy it farmed or wild, and stays moist with this herb dressing.

4	salmon steaks (2 lb/1 kg), 1 inch (2.5 cm) thick	4
1 lb	asparagus	500 g
HERB VINAIGRETTE:		
3 tbsp	olive oil	50 mL
4 tsp	tarragon vinegar	20 mL
½ tsp	Dijon mustard	2 mL
Pinch	granulated sugar	Pinch
1 tbsp	each chopped fresh tarragon and chives	15 mL

- HERB VINAIGRETTE: In small bowl, whisk together oil, vinegar, mustard and sugar; stir in tarragon and chives. Brush salmon all over with 2 tbsp (25 mL) of the vinaigrette.

- Place salmon and asparagus on greased grill over medium heat. Cover and cook, turning salmon once and asparagus often, for 8 to 10 minutes or until fish flakes easily when tested with fork and asparagus is tender-crisp. Spoon remaining vinaigrette over both.

Makes 4 servings.

PER SERVING: about 385 calories, 43 g protein, 21 g fat, 4 g carbohydrate, good source iron.

Fish Sticks with Crunchy Coating

Chef Kate Gammal's toddlers love fish sticks, so she keeps this coating on hand. It has just the right amount of crunch without adding fat or preservatives and works just as well with strips of chicken or turkey breast.

6 oz	white fish fillet	175 g
¼ cup	all-purpose flour	50 mL
1	egg	1
1 tbsp	water	15 mL
½ cup	Crunchy Coating (recipe follows)	125 mL

- Cut fish into 3-inch (8 cm) long 1-inch (2.5 cm) thick strips; set aside. Place flour in shallow dish. In another shallow dish, combine egg and water. Place Crunchy Coating in third dish.
- A few pieces at a time, press fish into flour, turning to coat; shake off excess. Dip into egg mixture, then into Crunchy Coating, turning to coat all over. Broil, turning once, for about 5 minutes or until fish flakes easily when tested with fork.

Makes 2 servings.
PER SERVING: about 290 calories, 25 g protein, 6 g fat, 30 g carbohydrate, good source iron.

CRUNCHY COATING

In airtight container, combine 1 cup (250 mL) dry bread crumbs, ½ cup (125 mL) coarsely crushed unsalted soda crackers, 1 tsp (5 mL) dried basil and ½ tsp (2 mL) each dried oregano, salt and pepper.

Makes 1 ½ cups (375 mL).
PER ½ CUP (125 mL): about 205 calories, 6 g protein, 3 g fat, 37 g carbohydrate.

Pan-Fried Fillets with Warm Tomato Mango Relish

Do you call this fresh dice of mango and tomato a relish, a salsa or a sauce? It swirls around in the pan just long enough to warm and blend flavors before saucing a golden flaky fillet.

1	large tomato, seeded and chopped	1
1	mango, chopped	1
½ cup	chopped red onion	125 mL
2 tbsp	chopped fresh coriander	25 mL
2 tsp	grated lime rind	10 mL
2 tbsp	lime juice	25 mL
Dash	hot pepper sauce	Dash
	Salt	
4	white fish fillets, ¾ inch (2 cm) thick (1 lb/500 g)	4
2 tsp	vegetable oil	10 mL
	Pepper	

- In bowl, stir together tomato, mango, onion, coriander, lime rind and juice, hot pepper sauce and ¼ tsp (1 mL) salt; set aside.
- Pat fish dry. Brush fish all over with oil; sprinkle with pinch each salt and pepper. In large nonstick skillet, cook fish over medium-high heat for about 2 minutes per side or until fish flakes easily when tested with fork. Transfer to warmed plates.
- Pour tomato mixture into pan; cook for about 15 seconds or just until warm. Serve over fish.

Makes 4 servings.
PER SERVING: about 180 calories, 22 g protein, 4 g fat, 13 g carbohydrate.

Saucy Mushroom Pork Chops

Not overcooking is the secret to moist and tender pork chops. Mushrooms, a classic addition, enrich the pork and make a sauce that's quick to prepare for a weeknight supper.

2 tsp	(approx) vegetable oil	10 mL
1 lb	fast-fry boneless pork chops, trimmed	500 g
½ tsp	dried rosemary	2 mL
¼ tsp	each dried thyme, salt and pepper	1 mL
1	onion, chopped	1
3 cups	sliced mushrooms (½ lb/250 g)	750 mL
1 tsp	cornstarch	5 mL
½ cup	chicken stock	125 mL

- In large skillet, heat oil over high heat; brown chops on 1 side, about 1½ minutes. Turn and sprinkle with half each of the rosemary, thyme, salt and pepper; brown second side. Set aside.
- Reduce heat to medium; add more oil if needed. Cook onion, mushrooms and remaining rosemary, thyme, salt and pepper, stirring occasionally, for 5 minutes or until most of the mushroom liquid is evaporated.
- Stir cornstarch into stock; add to skillet. Bring to boil; cook, stirring, for 1 minute or until thickened. Add chops and any juices on plate; cook for 2 minutes or until tender yet still slightly pink inside.

Makes 4 servings.
PER SERVING: about 215 calories, 27 g protein, 9 g fat, 5 g carbohydrate.

Cranberry Orange Ham Steaks

Don't forget how good ham is for quick suppers. It's usually lean and very well trimmed. Because of its smokiness, it's particularly tasty, so a little goes a long way.

¼ cup	frozen Cranberry Cocktail concentrate, thawed	50 mL
1 tsp	grated orange rind	5 mL
1 tsp	Dijon mustard	5 mL
6	cooked ham steaks (about 1 ½ lb / 750 g)	6

- In small bowl, combine cranberry concentrate, orange rind and mustard; set aside.
- Place ham steaks on greased grill over medium-high heat; cover and cook, turning once, for about 10 minutes or until heated through. Brush both sides with glaze; cook for 1 minute, turning once.

Makes 6 servings.
PER SERVING: about 180 calories, 21 g protein, 7 g fat, 6 g carbohydrate.

TIP: Ham steaks cost more per pound (kilogram) than a small smoked ham. Buy one of these, then cut it up into ½-inch (1 cm) thick steaks. Use any leftover ham for sandwiches, salads or casseroles.

Oriental Beef and Noodle Stir-Fry

Lean ground beef is a good choice for this sort of dish in which you can tip the skillet and skim off any fat. If you use a nonstick skillet, you may not need any oil to start the dish.

2 tsp	vegetable oil	10 mL
1 tbsp	minced gingerroot	15 mL
1	clove garlic, minced	1
1	onion, sliced	1
1 lb	lean ground beef	500 g
1½ cups	beef stock	375 mL
⅓ cup	oyster sauce	75 mL
2 tbsp	each soy sauce and rice vinegar	25 mL
1 tbsp	packed brown sugar	15 mL
2	carrots, sliced	2
1	pkg (450 g) precooked spaghetti-style Chinese noodles	1
1	sweet red pepper, julienned	1
1 tbsp	cornstarch	15 mL
1½ cups	snow peas	375 mL
	Salt and pepper	

- In wok or large deep skillet, heat oil over high heat; stir-fry ginger, garlic and onion for 30 seconds. Add beef; stir-fry, breaking up meat, for 4 minutes or until no longer pink. Skim off any fat.

- Combine stock, oyster sauce, soy sauce, vinegar and sugar. Add to wok along with carrots; bring to boil.

- Tear noodles apart and add to wok; cook, stirring, over medium-high heat for 2 minutes. Add red pepper and cook, stirring, for 3 minutes.

- Dissolve cornstarch in 1 tbsp (15 mL) water; stir into wok and cook, stirring, for 1 minute or until thickened. Stir in snow peas; cook for 2 minutes or until tender-crisp. Season with salt and pepper to taste.

Makes 4 servings.
PER SERVING: about 665 calories, 38 g protein, 20 g fat, 81 g carbohydrate, very high source fibre, excellent source iron.

Vegetable Beef Stir-Fry for One

Heap hot cooked rice into a bowl to top with this quick and easy stir-fry.

1 tsp	vegetable oil	5 mL
¼ lb	lean boneless beef, cut in thin strips	125 g
2	green onions, sliced	2
2	small carrots, thinly sliced	2
1 tsp	minced gingerroot	5 mL
Half	clove garlic, chopped	Half
1 cup	sliced mushrooms	250 mL
1 tsp	cornstarch	5 mL
2 tsp	soy sauce	10 mL
½ tsp	oyster sauce	2 mL
1 cup	bean sprouts	250 mL
	Salt and pepper	

- In nonstick skillet or wok, heat oil over medium-high heat; stir-fry beef until browned. Transfer to plate and set aside.

- Add onions, carrots, ginger and garlic to skillet; stir-fry for 30 seconds. Add mushrooms; stir-fry for 1 minute. Stir in ¼ cup (50 mL) water. Reduce heat to medium; cover and cook for 3 minutes.

- In small bowl, blend cornstarch into 1 tbsp (15 mL) cold water; stir in soy sauce and oyster sauce. Return beef to skillet; stir in cornstarch mixture. Cook, stirring, for 2 minutes or until thickened and beef is hot. Stir in bean sprouts. Season with salt and pepper to taste.

Makes 1 serving.

PER SERVING: about 305 calories, 31 g protein, 10 g fat, 25 g carbohydrate, very high source fibre, excellent source iron.

Red Pepper and Tofu Stir-Fry

Tofu is the answer to your dreams if you dream about cooking a quick and really delicious vegetarian entrée. Serve with rice and steamed spinach, green beans or sugar snap peas.

½ lb	firm tofu	250 g
½ cup	vegetable stock or water	125 mL
1 tbsp	soy sauce	15 mL
1 tbsp	oyster sauce	15 mL
1 tsp	cider vinegar	5 mL
½ tsp	sesame oil	2 mL
¼ tsp	granulated sugar	1 mL
Dash	hot pepper sauce	Dash
1 tsp	cornstarch	5 mL
1	sweet red pepper	1
2	green onions	2
½ cup	snow peas	125 mL
1 tsp	sesame seeds	5 mL
2 tsp	vegetable oil	10 mL
2 tsp	minced gingerroot	10 mL
1	clove garlic, minced	1

- Cut tofu into ½-inch (1 cm) cubes; place in shallow dish. Whisk together stock, soy sauce, oyster sauce, vinegar, sesame oil, sugar and hot pepper sauce; pour over tofu. Let stand for 20 minutes. Drain, reserving marinade; set tofu aside. Whisk cornstarch into marinade; set aside.

- Cut red pepper into strips. Cut green onions diagonally into 2-inch (5 cm) long strips. Trim snow peas.

- Heat wok or deep skillet over medium heat; cook sesame seeds for 2 minutes or until golden. Set aside.

- Add oil to pan; increase heat to medium-high. Stir-fry ginger and garlic for 10 seconds. Add red pepper; stir-fry for 1 minute. Add tofu; stir-fry for 3 minutes. Add snow peas and onions; stir-fry for 30 seconds.

- Push tofu mixture to side of pan. Pour in cornstarch mixture; cook, stirring, for 1 to 2 minutes or until thickened. Stir tofu mixture back into sauce; sprinkle with sesame seeds.

Makes 2 servings.

PER SERVING: about 280 calories, 20 g protein, 17 g fat, 17 g carbohydrate, high source fibre, good source calcium, excellent source iron.

Tasty Oven Chicken Fingers

For supper or a birthday party, serve these light crispy fingers hot with Honey Garlic Dipping Sauce (recipe below). For great picnic fare, cool on a rack before serving.

1 cup	fine cornflake crumbs	250 mL
⅓ cup	freshly grated Parmesan cheese	75 mL
1 tbsp	finely chopped fresh parsley	15 mL
½ tsp	paprika	2 mL
¼ tsp	each salt and pepper	1 mL
1	egg	1
1	egg white	1
1	clove garlic, minced	1
6	boneless skinless chicken breasts	6

- In plastic bag, shake together cornflake crumbs, Parmesan cheese, parsley, paprika, salt and pepper. In shallow dish, whisk together egg, egg white and garlic.

- Cut chicken lengthwise into ¾-inch (2 cm) wide strips. One at a time, dip strips into egg mixture, then shake in crumb mixture until evenly coated. Place on greased baking sheet.

- Bake in 400°F (200°C) oven for 5 minutes or until no longer pink inside.

Makes 6 servings.
PER SERVING: about 245 calories, 33 g protein, 4 g fat, 17 g carbohydrate, excellent source iron.

HONEY GARLIC DIPPING SAUCE

In small bowl, stir together ¼ cup (50 mL) liquid honey, 3 tbsp (50 mL) chicken stock, 1 tbsp (15 mL) soy sauce, 1 minced clove garlic and dash hot pepper sauce. Let stand for 1 hour. *(Sauce can be covered and refrigerated for up to 1 week.)*

Makes ½ cup (125 mL).
PER 2 TBSP (25 mL): about 70 calories, 1 g protein, trace fat, 18 g carbohydrate.

Chicken Thyme Toss for Two

A big complaint of small households is dealing with leftovers. This recipe solves the problem deliciously.

2	chicken legs	2
2 tbsp	all-purpose flour	25 mL
2 tsp	dried thyme	10 mL
¼ tsp	each salt and pepper	1 mL
2 tsp	vegetable oil	10 mL
⅓ cup	sliced carrot	75 mL
1	onion, chopped	1
1	clove garlic, minced	1
1½ cups	chicken stock	375 mL
⅔ cup	pasta shells	150 mL
⅓ cup	snow peas, sliced crosswise, or frozen peas	75 mL

- Pull off skin from chicken; separate legs at joint. In bowl, stir together flour, thyme, salt and pepper; add chicken and toss to coat.

- In skillet, heat oil over medium-high heat; cook chicken, turning once, for 5 to 7 minutes or until browned. Transfer to plate and set aside.

- Reduce heat to medium. Add carrot, onion and garlic to pan; cook, stirring to scrape up brown bits, for 5 to 6 minutes or until softened. Pour in chicken stock and pasta; bring to boil.

- Return chicken to pan; cover and simmer for 25 minutes or until juices run clear when chicken is pierced and pasta is tender but firm. Stir in peas; cook for 2 minutes or until hot.

Makes 2 servings.
PER SERVING: about 420 calories, 36 g protein, 11 g fat, 40 g carbohydrate, high source fibre, excellent source iron.

Grilled Pepper Steak Sandwiches

A quick spread replaces a marinade to expand the flavors of steak on the grill.

1 lb	sirloin steak, 1-inch (2.5 cm) thick	500 g
1	each small sweet red, green and yellow pepper, sliced	1
2	green onions, chopped	2
1	clove garlic, minced	1
1 tbsp	chopped fresh basil (or 1 tsp/5 mL dried)	15 mL
1 tbsp	olive oil	15 mL
Pinch	each salt and pepper	Pinch
4	crusty rolls	4
MUSTARD HERB MIX:		
1 tbsp	Dijon mustard	15 mL
1 tsp	dried oregano	5 mL
1	clove garlic, minced	1
½ tsp	pepper	2 mL

- MUSTARD HERB MIX: Combine mustard, oregano, garlic and pepper. Trim fat from steak; spread mustard mix onto each side.

- Place red, green and yellow peppers, onions, garlic and basil in centre of large piece of heavy-duty foil; toss together lightly. Sprinkle with oil, salt and pepper. Fold up foil to form package, sealing well.

- Place steak and package on greased grill over high heat. Cook steak, turning once, for 10 minutes for medium-rare or to desired doneness; cook package until puffed. Remove steak to cutting board; tent with foil and let stand for 5 minutes.

- Slice each roll in half horizontally, without cutting completely through. Slice steak and stack onto rolls; top with pepper mixture.

Makes 4 servings.
PER SERVING: about 385 calories, 28 g protein, 11 g fat, 43 g carbohydrate, excellent source iron.

Chicken Avocado Heroes

Sandwiches ease into dinnertime as satisfying main courses, especially if they feature grilled chicken.

4	boneless skinless chicken breasts	4
Pinch	each salt and pepper	Pinch
4	thin slices Danbo or other firm low-fat cheese	4
1	tomato	1
1	ripe avocado	1
4	kaiser or onion rolls	4
2 tbsp	light mayonnaise	25 mL
1 tsp	Dijon mustard	5 mL
4	lettuce leaves	4

TIP: A ridged cast-iron skillet is an excellent year-round grill. You can cook chops, ham steaks, burgers and fish fillets with little or no fat. The ridged pan, set over any element, gives the food grill marks and a real taste of summer.

- Place chicken between sheets of waxed paper; pound lightly to flatten. Sprinkle with salt and pepper.

- Place on greased grill over medium-high heat; cover and cook for 6 minutes. Turn and top with cheese; cook for 5 to 6 minutes or until cheese is melted and chicken is no longer pink inside.

- Meanwhile, cut tomato into 8 slices. Peel, quarter and pit avocado; slice thinly lengthwise, without cutting completely through, to form fans.

- Slice each roll in half horizontally, without cutting completely through; open and toast lightly on grill.

- Mix together mayonnaise and mustard; spread over bottom half of each bun. Top each with lettuce leaf, 2 slices tomato, chicken breast and avocado fan. Close bun, pressing lightly.

Makes 4 servings.
PER SERVING: about 515 calories, 41 g protein, 17 g fat, 45 g carbohydrate, good source calcium and iron.

Grilled Sausage Sandwiches

Adjust the spiciness of this hearty sandwich from mild to zippy by using either sweet or hot sausage. Alongside this casual entrée, serve crunchy vegetables.

1 tbsp	olive oil	15 mL
1	onion, chopped	1
1	clove garlic, minced	1
1	sweet red pepper, coarsely chopped	1
Pinch	hot pepper flakes	Pinch
1	can (19 oz/540 mL) Italian Spice Stewed Tomatoes	1
2 tbsp	chopped fresh parsley	25 mL
¼ tsp	each salt and pepper	1 mL
4	Italian sausages (about 1 lb/500 g)	4
4	crusty Italian rolls	4
4	lettuce leaves	4
4 tsp	freshly grated Parmesan cheese	20 mL

- In heavy saucepan, heat oil over medium heat; cook onion and garlic, stirring occasionally, for 5 minutes or until softened. Add red pepper and hot pepper flakes; cook for 2 minutes.

- Stir in tomatoes, parsley, salt and pepper; bring to boil. Reduce heat; simmer for 20 minutes or until thickened.

- Meanwhile, cut sausages lengthwise almost all the way through. Open and place, cut side down, on greased grill over medium-high heat; cook for about 5 minutes per side or until crisp on outside and no longer pink inside.

- Slice each roll in half horizontally; toast, cut side down, for 2 to 3 minutes or until just golden. Top each bottom half with lettuce and sausage; spoon tomato sauce over top. Sprinkle with Parmesan; cover with top half of roll.

Makes 4 servings.
PER SERVING: about 505 calories, 26 g protein, 22 g fat, 52 g carbohydrate, high source fibre, excellent source iron.

Bean Soup with Carrot Salsa

What a difference this simple grated carrot salsa makes to a healthy, almost instant bean soup. It zaps the mild-flavored purée with crunch and taste tingles. Serve with toasted pita triangles.

1 tsp	vegetable oil	5 mL
1	onion, chopped	1
2	cloves garlic, minced	2
¾ tsp	each ground cumin and coriander	4 mL
2	cans (each 19 oz/540 mL) white kidney beans, drained and rinsed	2
3 cups	vegetable or chicken stock	750 mL
	Salt and pepper	
Carrot Salsa:		
1	carrot, grated	1
4 tsp	chopped fresh coriander or parsley	20 mL
1 tsp	lemon juice	5 mL
½ tsp	vegetable oil	2 mL

- In saucepan, heat oil over medium heat; cook onion and garlic, stirring occasionally, for 3 minutes or until softened. Add cumin and ground coriander; cook for 1 minute.
- Add kidney beans and stock; bring to boil. Reduce heat, cover and simmer for 15 minutes.
- Carrot Salsa: Meanwhile, in bowl, stir together carrot, fresh coriander, lemon juice and oil; set aside.
- In food processor or blender, purée soup until smooth; if necessary, return to saucepan and heat through. Season with salt and pepper to taste. Serve topped with carrot salsa.

Makes 4 servings.
Per serving: about 275 calories, 17 g protein, 4 g fat, 47 g carbohydrate, very high source fibre, good source iron.

Quick Gazpacho for One

*Pamper yourself with this refreshing hot-weather soup.
For a change, try vegetable cocktail instead of tomato juice.*

2	tomatoes, peeled, seeded and chopped	2
⅓ cup	tomato juice	75 mL
2 tbsp	chopped celery	25 mL
Half	clove garlic, minced	Half
⅓ cup	chopped seedless cucumber	75 mL
¼ cup	chopped sweet green pepper	50 mL
2	green onions, sliced	2
Dash	hot pepper sauce	Dash
Pinch	salt	Pinch

- In blender or food processor, combine tomatoes, tomato juice, celery, garlic, half of the cucumber, half of the green pepper and half of the onions, the hot pepper sauce and salt until vegetables are finely chopped but not puréed.
- Stir in remaining cucumber, green pepper and onions. Refrigerate until chilled.

Makes 1 serving.
Per serving: about 85 calories, 4 g protein, 1 g fat, 19 g carbohydrate, high source fibre, good source iron.

Tip: On cool nights, heat the soup just to boiling and serve hot with croutons or crackers.

Pasta Spinach Soup

Homemade soup for dinner sounds like a grand idea. But what if you haven't been simmering that stockpot all day? Take heart and try this robust half-hour soup that relies on good-quality canned broth. Serve with slices of crisp garlic bread, topped bruschetta-style with chopped tomatoes and basil.

2	carrots	2
1	large potato, peeled	1
1	onion	1
1	stalk celery	1
2 tbsp	olive oil	25 mL
1	clove garlic, minced	1
¼ tsp	dried rosemary	1 mL
½ cup	broken spaghetti	125 mL
2	cans (each 10 oz/284 mL) chicken stock	2
5 cups	packed fresh spinach (half 10 oz/284 g pkg)	1.25 L
	Freshly grated Parmesan cheese	

- Cut carrots, potato, onion and celery into bite-size chunks. In large saucepan, heat oil over medium heat; cook vegetables, garlic and rosemary, covered, stirring occasionally, for 5 minutes.

- Stir in spaghetti, then chicken stock and 2 stock cans of water; bring to boil. Boil gently for about 15 minutes or until noodles and vegetables are tender.

- Stack spinach leaves; slice into thin strips. Stir into soup; heat for about 1 minute or just until wilted. Serve sprinkled with Parmesan.

Makes 4 servings.

PER SERVING: about 250 calories, 11 g protein, 9 g fat, 31 g carbohydrate, good source iron.

Elizabeth Baird's Mushroom Barley Salad

Mushrooms and barley are familiar partners in a baked side dish, but here they get together with new vigor for an all-season salad.

2¼ cups	water	550 mL
¾ cup	pot or pearl barley	175 mL
2	carrots, thinly sliced	2
3 cups	sliced mushrooms (½ lb/250 g)	750 mL
3	green onions, sliced	3
½ cup	diced sweet red pepper	125 mL
¼ cup	minced fresh parsley	50 mL
¼ cup	corn kernels	50 mL
¼ cup	diced celery	50 mL
DRESSING:		
⅓ cup	cider vinegar	75 mL
⅓ cup	vegetable oil	75 mL
2 tsp	Dijon mustard	10 mL
1½ tsp	dried thyme	7 mL
¾ tsp	each salt and pepper	4 mL

- In saucepan, bring water and barley to boil; reduce heat, cover and simmer for 25 minutes.

- Add carrots; cook for about 15 minutes or until barley is tender and most of the liquid is absorbed. Drain well in sieve.

- DRESSING: Meanwhile, in large bowl, combine vinegar, oil, mustard, thyme, salt and pepper; add barley mixture and toss with fork. Let cool. *(Salad can be prepared to this point, covered and refrigerated for up to 24 hours.)*

- Add mushrooms, onions, red pepper, parsley, corn and celery; toss gently.

Makes 6 servings.
PER SERVING: about 235 calories, 3 g protein, 13 g fat, 28 g carbohydrate.

VARIATION
MUSHROOM RICE SALAD: Substitute parboiled white rice or whole grain rice for barley. Cook in 1½ cups (375 mL) water for about 20 minutes for white, 35 for whole grain, and adding carrots 15 minutes before the end.

Sesame Spinach Salad

When choosing greens for a salad, spinach should top your list. Unlike a lot of lettuces on the market, it has taste, and the dark green color means it's rich in valuable beta-carotene.

1	pkg (10 oz/284 g) fresh spinach	1
4	thin slices red onion	4
1 tbsp	sesame seeds	15 mL
2 tbsp	white wine vinegar or rice vinegar	25 mL
1 tbsp	light soy sauce	15 mL
2 tsp	granulated sugar	10 mL
3 tbsp	vegetable oil	50 mL
1 tsp	sesame oil	5 mL

- Trim spinach and tear into pieces to make about 10 cups (2.5 L) lightly packed; arrange in large salad bowl. Separate onion into rings; scatter over spinach.

- In microwaveable measure or skillet, toast sesame seeds at High or over medium-high heat until golden, about 3 minutes; set aside.

- In bowl, stir together vinegar, soy sauce and sugar until sugar dissolves; whisk in vegetable and sesame oils. Pour over spinach mixture. Sprinkle with sesame seeds and toss well.

Makes 6 servings.
PER SERVING: about 95 calories, 2 g protein, 8 g fat, 4 g carbohydrate.

TIP: Salad and dressing can each be prepared ahead; cover spinach with damp tea towel and dressing with plastic wrap and chill for up to 2 hours.

A Toss of Greens with Dressing

Meals in the fast lane do require some planning. For example, salad is a quick side dish as long as the lettuce is washed and spun dry immediately after shopping. To keep it crisp as long as possible, wrap it in towels, then place in plastic bag.

½ cup	low-fat cottage cheese	125 mL
2 tbsp	milk	25 mL
1 tsp	dried mint leaves	5 mL
1 tsp	lemon juice	5 mL
½ tsp	Dijon mustard	2 mL
Pinch	granulated sugar	Pinch
	Salt and pepper	
8 cups	shredded or torn salad greens	2 L
2	green onions, sliced	2
¼ cup	sliced radishes	50 mL

- In blender, purée together cottage cheese, milk, mint, lemon juice, mustard, sugar, and salt and pepper to taste.
- Arrange salad greens and onions in bowls; pour dressing over top. Garnish with radishes.

Makes 4 servings.
PER SERVING: about 55 calories, 6 g protein, 1 g fat, 6 g carbohydrate.

Vegetable Cracked Wheat Pilaf

Cracked wheat has much more fibre than rice or pasta and an intriguing nutty flavor. Serve as a side dish with a salad and grilled fish. If leeks are not available, substitute onions.

1½ tsp	vegetable oil	7 mL
1½ cups	coarsely chopped mushrooms	375 mL
2	small leeks (white and light green parts), coarsely chopped	2
1 cup	cracked wheat	250 mL
1½ cups	boiling water	375 mL
1	carrot, thinly sliced	1
1 cup	chopped green beans	250 mL
¼ cup	sunflower seeds	50 mL
	Salt and pepper	

- In Dutch oven or large heavy saucepan, heat oil over medium heat; cook mushrooms and leeks, stirring occasionally, for 5 to 8 minutes or until leeks are tender.
- Stir in cracked wheat; cook, stirring, for 2 minutes. Pour in water; cover and simmer over low heat for 5 minutes. Add carrot; cook, covered, for 5 minutes. Add green beans; cook, covered, for 10 to 15 minutes or until all vegetables are tender.
- Meanwhile, in skillet, toast sunflower seeds, stirring occasionally, for 5 minutes or until golden. Sprinkle over pilaf; season with salt and pepper to taste. Serve hot.

Makes 5 servings.
PER SERVING: about 180 calories, 6 g protein, 5 g fat, 29 g carbohydrate, very high source fibre, good source iron.

> TIP: Cracked wheat is made from the wheat kernels known as "wheat berries" broken into coarse, medium or fine fragments. Available in bulk and health food stores.

Mushroom Lentil Burgers

Inspired by the vegetarian burgers available in most supermarkets, home economist Jennifer MacKenzie created these homemade burgers. They're almost embarrassingly inexpensive and superior-tasting.

1 tsp	vegetable oil	5 mL
1	onion, finely chopped	1
1 cup	finely chopped mushrooms	250 mL
½ tsp	dried thyme	2 mL
1	can (19 oz/540 mL) lentils, drained and rinsed	1
½ cup	quick-cooking rolled oats	125 mL
3 tbsp	freshly grated Parmesan cheese	50 mL
2 tbsp	chopped pine nuts or pecans	25 mL
¼ tsp	pepper	1 mL
4	lettuce leaves	4
4	poppy seed hamburger buns	4

- In nonstick skillet, heat oil over medium heat; cook onion, stirring, for 4 minutes or until softened. Add mushrooms and thyme; cook, stirring, for 4 minutes or just until starting to brown. Let cool slightly.

- In bowl, mash lentils coarsely; stir in mushroom mixture, rolled oats, cheese, pine nuts and pepper. Shape into four ¾-inch (2 cm) thick patties.

- In skillet or on greased grill, cook patties over medium-high heat for 3 to 4 minutes per side or until golden brown. Sandwich with lettuce in buns.

Makes 4 servings.
PER SERVING: about 410 calories, 20 g protein, 10 g fat, 63 g carbohydrate, very high source fibre, excellent source iron.

Pronto Couscous Pilaf

Parsley and lemon brighten the taste of couscous, while sweet green or red pepper adds color. Serve as a side dish with quick-cooking entrées such as broiled or grilled chicken and fish.

2 tsp	vegetable oil	10 mL
4	green onions, chopped	4
1	sweet green or red pepper, finely diced	1
¾ tsp	salt	4 mL
¼ tsp	each pepper and cinnamon	1 mL
2¼ cups	water	550 mL
1½ cups	couscous	375 mL
¼ cup	chopped fresh parsley	50 mL
1 tbsp	lemon juice	15 mL

- In saucepan, heat oil over medium heat; cook onions, green pepper, salt, pepper and cinnamon, stirring occasionally, for about 3 minutes or until vegetables are softened.
- Pour in water; bring to boil. Stir in couscous, parsley and lemon juice; cover and remove from heat. Let stand for 5 minutes; fluff with fork.

Makes 6 servings.
PER SERVING: about 200 calories, 6 g protein, 2 g fat, 38 g carbohydrate.

TIP: Couscous is granular semolina (ground Durum wheat), a staple of North African cooking and the newest, quickest starch on the block in North America. Available in bulk and health food stores, or in supermarkets, boxed, at a higher price.

Baked Potato with Asparagus Topping

Few foods are as wholesome as potatoes, which contain complex carbohydrates, protein and ample vitamins and minerals. And with the help of a microwave, they make a fast and satisfying meal for one.

1	large baking potato	1
1 tsp	vegetable oil	5 mL
1 tbsp	chopped onion	15 mL
4	stalks asparagus, cut diagonally in 1-inch (2.5) lengths	4
Half	small carrot, thinly sliced	Half
3 tbsp	light sour cream	50 mL
	Pepper and salt	

TIP: For 2 servings, double ingredients. If microwaving 2 potatoes at once, add 2 or 3 minutes to cooking time.

- Scrub potato; prick several times with fork. Microwave at High, turning once, for about 5 minutes or until tender. Wrap in paper towel; let stand for 5 minutes. (Or bake potato in 425°F/220°C oven or toaster oven for 1 hour or until tender.)
- Meanwhile, in small saucepan, heat oil over medium heat; cook onion, asparagus and carrot, stirring, for about 4 minutes or until tender-crisp. Reduce heat to low. Stir in sour cream, and pepper to taste; heat through.
- Cut potato in half and mash pulp with fork; season with salt and pepper to taste. Spoon asparagus mixture over potato.

Makes 1 serving.
PER SERVING: about 295 calories, 9 g protein, 7 g fat, 51 g carbohydrate, very high source fibre, good source iron.

Crispy Sweet Potato Wedges

Lightly breaded, herb-flecked, crispy on the outside and creamy inside, these potato wedges are a nifty alternative to french fries.

3	sweet potatoes (about 2 ½ lb/1.25 kg)	3
1	egg	1
1	clove garlic, minced	1
½ cup	dry bread crumbs	125 mL
½ cup	freshly grated Parmesan cheese	125 mL
1 tsp	each dried basil and oregano	5 mL

TIP: Sweet potatoes are one of the most nutrient-dense foods we can eat. Even though they're called "sweet," they have about the same calories as white potatoes and contain more beta-carotene than a carrot. A 5-inch (12 cm) long sweet potato supplies almost half the daily requirement for vitamin C along with significant amounts of fibre. Sweet potatoes are now being grown in Canada on former tobacco lands near Simcoe, Ontario.

- Peel potatoes; cut each lengthwise into 8 wedges. In large bowl, whisk together egg, garlic and 1 tbsp (15 mL) water. Add potatoes; toss to coat evenly.

- In shallow dish, combine bread crumbs, Parmesan cheese, basil and oregano; roll potato wedges in mixture to coat well.

- Bake on greased baking sheet in 425°F (220°C) oven for 15 minutes. Turn wedges; bake for 12 to 15 minutes longer or until potatoes are tender.

Makes 4 servings.
PER SERVING: about 395 calories, 13 g protein, 6 g fat, 72 g carbohydrate, very high source fibre, good source calcium and iron.

Herb and Sesame Broccoli

Broccoli comes in prime condition all year, and it's a gold mine of vitamin C and beta-carotene.
With this nutty sesame treatment, it's hard to resist.

1	bunch broccoli (about 1 lb/500 g)	1
1 tsp	dried basil	5 mL
¼ tsp	salt	1 mL
1 tbsp	sesame or olive oil	15 mL
2 tsp	sesame seeds	10 mL
	Pepper	

• Divide broccoli into florets; slice stalks thinly on the diagonal. Place in steamer set over boiling water; sprinkle with basil and salt. Cover and steam for 3 to 5 minutes or until tender-crisp.

• Remove steamer basket and set aside. Drain pan and return to medium heat to dry. Add oil and sesame seeds; cook for 1 minute or until golden. Add broccoli and toss for 30 seconds. Season with pepper to taste.

Makes 4 servings.
PER SERVING: about 65 calories, 3 g protein, 5 g fat, 5 g carbohydrate.

Mushroom and Onion Combo

Cook this comfy steak-loving duo on the barbecue or in a covered casserole in the oven.

12 cups	mushrooms, halved (about 2 lb/1kg)	3 L
1	onion, thinly sliced	1
¼ cup	chopped fresh basil (or 4 tsp/20 mL dried)	50 mL
1 tbsp	butter, melted	15 mL
1 tbsp	balsamic or red wine vinegar	15 mL
½ tsp	each salt and pepper	2 mL

• In bowl, toss together mushrooms, onion, basil, butter, vinegar, salt and pepper. Arrange on large piece of double-thickness heavy-duty foil; fold up sides and seal tightly to form packet.

• Place on grill over medium-high heat; cook for about 30 minutes or until mushrooms and onions are tender and light golden.

Makes 6 servings.
PER SERVING: about 55 calories, 3 g protein, 2 g fat, 7 g carbohydrate.

Green Beans with Sweet Red Pepper

Taking care and being creative with even the simplest ingredients, such as green beans, is a sign of a good cook.
Here, diced sweet red pepper and sesame oil add spark to taste and presentation.

½ lb	green beans, trimmed	250 g
¼ cup	diced sweet red pepper	50 mL
2 tbsp	toasted sesame seeds	25 mL
½ tsp	each sesame oil and lemon juice	2 mL
	Salt and pepper	

• In saucepan of boiling water, cook green beans for 4 minutes or just until tender-crisp; drain well.

• Toss beans with red pepper, sesame seeds, sesame oil, lemon juice, and salt and pepper to taste.

Makes 2 servings.
PER SERVING: about 100 calories, 4 g protein, 7 g fat, 10 g carbohydrate.

CHAPTER TWO

SLOW AND EASY SIMMERS

What an antidote to the rush of our lives — a pot simmering with soup or bubbling lazily with a robust stew, flavors mingling and marrying as they only can with time and gentle heat. Let the aromas take over your kitchen, offering a welcome to one and all.

New Chicken Stew

What's new is the lighter touch with skinned chicken and the warm Mediterranean flavors that come from the fennel, bay leaf, thyme and sweet pepper. Crusty bread is a must accompaniment.

4	chicken legs, skinned	4
3	cloves garlic, minced	3
2	onions, chopped	2
2	bay leaves	2
1	sweet red pepper, diced	1
1	fennel bulb or celery heart, chopped	1
1 tsp	dried thyme	5 mL
½ tsp	paprika	2 mL
¼ tsp	hot pepper flakes	1 mL
Pinch	turmeric	Pinch
1 tbsp	olive oil	15 mL
2 cups	chicken stock	500 mL
2	large tomatoes, chopped	2
8	new potatoes (1 lb/500 g)	8
½ tsp	each salt and pepper	2 mL

GARLIC SAUCE (OPTIONAL):

1	clove garlic, minced	1
⅓ cup	light mayonnaise	75 mL
1 tsp	tomato paste	5 mL
1 tsp	lemon juice	5 mL
Pinch	cayenne pepper	Pinch

- Separate chicken legs at joint; place in glass bowl. Add garlic, onions, bay leaves, red pepper, fennel, thyme, paprika, hot pepper flakes and turmeric; toss well. Cover and refrigerate for at least 4 hours or up to 12 hours.

- GARLIC SAUCE (if using): Meanwhile, in small bowl and using fork, crush garlic; blend in mayonnaise, tomato paste, lemon juice and cayenne. Cover and refrigerate for up to 1 day.

- Remove chicken from vegetable mixture, brushing off mixture. In large nonstick skillet, heat oil over medium-high heat; brown chicken on all sides, about 10 minutes. Transfer to plate.

- Reduce heat to medium-low. Add vegetable mixture to skillet; cook, stirring often, for about 10 minutes or until softened.

- Return chicken to skillet. Add stock, tomatoes and potatoes; bring to boil. Reduce heat to medium-low; cover and simmer for about 25 minutes or until juices run clear when chicken is pierced and potatoes are tender. Discard bay leaves. Season with salt and pepper. Serve garnished with garlic sauce.

Makes 4 servings.
PER SERVING (without garlic sauce): about 355 calories, 33 g protein, 10 g fat, 35 g carbohydrate, high source fibre, excellent source iron.

Homemade Chicken Stock

Chicken backs and necks, always a bargain, lay the foundation for a rich chicken stock.

3 lb	chicken backs and necks	1.5 kg
1	onion	1
4	whole cloves	4
4	sprigs fresh parsley	4
1	each stalk celery and carrot, chopped	1
1 tsp	dried thyme	5 mL
1	bay leaf	1

- In large saucepan, combine 12 cups (3 L) cold water, chicken bones, onion, cloves, parsley, celery, carrot, thyme and bay leaf; bring to boil. Skim foam from top. Reduce heat and simmer for 1½ hours.

- Strain and refrigerate stock until jelled, about 8 hours. Remove and discard fat from surface.

Makes about 8½ cups (2.125 L).
PER 1 CUP (250 mL): about 40 calories, 5 g protein, 1 g fat, 1 g carbohydrate.

Braised Lamb and Onions

Onions build the flavor for a hearty stew. Try it with potatoes mashed with buttermilk and either steamed broccoli or green beans.

2½ lb	lean lamb, trimmed	1.25 kg
2 tbsp	olive oil	25 mL
6	large onions, cut in wedges	6
5	cloves garlic, slivered	5
4	large carrots, cut in chunks	4
1 tsp	paprika	5 mL
2 cups	chicken stock	500 mL
1 cup	dry white wine or chicken stock	250 mL
1 tbsp	tomato paste	15 mL
½ tsp	salt	2 mL
¼ tsp	pepper	1 mL
2 tbsp	butter, softened	25 mL
2 tbsp	all-purpose flour	25 mL
¼ cup	chopped fresh parsley	50 mL

- Cut lamb into ¾-inch (2 cm) cubes. In Dutch oven, heat half of the oil over high heat; brown lamb, in batches and adding more oil if necessary. Remove lamb to plate and set aside.

- Add remaining oil to pan; cook onions, garlic, carrots and paprika over medium-low heat, stirring occasionally, for 6 minutes or until slightly softened.

- Return lamb and any juices to pan; stir in stock, wine, tomato paste, salt and pepper. Bring to boil; reduce heat, cover and simmer for about 1½ hours or until lamb is tender, stirring occasionally.

- Blend butter with flour and stir into pan juices; cook, stirring, for 5 minutes or until thickened and smooth. Sprinkle with parsley.

Makes 6 servings.

PER SERVING: about 450 calories, 43 g protein, 21 g fat, 22 g carbohydrate, high source fibre, excellent source iron.

Basque Pork Stew

Citrusy chunks of succulent lean pork bring a little sunshine to the dinner table in this make-ahead stew.

2 lb	lean pork shoulder	1 kg
3 tbsp	olive oil	50 mL
	Salt and pepper	
2	onions, thickly sliced	2
1 cup	chicken stock	250 mL
2 tbsp	tomato paste	25 mL
2	sweet red peppers, cut in strips	2
¼ lb	prosciutto or ham, coarsely chopped	125 g
10	cloves garlic, thinly sliced	10
1 tsp	each paprika and dried thyme	5 mL
¼ tsp	hot pepper flakes	1 mL
1	orange	1

- Cut pork into 1½-inch (4 cm) cubes. In deep skillet or shallow saucepan, heat 1 tbsp (15 mL) of the oil over medium-high heat; brown pork, in batches and adding oil as necessary. Season with salt and pepper to taste. Transfer to plate and set aside.

- Add onions; cook over medium heat, stirring occasionally, for 5 minutes. Add stock and tomato paste; bring to boil, stirring to scrape up any brown bits. Return pork to skillet; stir in red peppers, prosciutto, garlic, paprika, thyme and hot pepper flakes.

- Grate rind from orange; add to stew. Peel orange; chop coarsely and stir into stew. Reduce heat; cover and simmer over low heat, stirring occasionally, for 1 to 1½ hours or until pork is tender. *(Stew can be cooled in refrigerator, covered and stored for up to 2 days. Or freeze for up to 2 months; thaw in refrigerator and reheat over medium-low heat.)*

Makes 4 servings.

PER SERVING: about 520 calories, 56 g protein, 24 g fat, 19 g carbohydrate, high source fibre, excellent source iron.

Lentil Stew on Coriander Couscous

Lentils are the answer to nutritious vegetarian meals.

1 cup	green lentils	250 mL
1 tbsp	vegetable oil	15 mL
1	onion, chopped	1
2	stalks celery, chopped	2
1	large sweet red pepper, chopped	1
2	cloves garlic, minced	2
1 tsp	minced gingerroot	5 mL
½ tsp	each ground coriander and cumin	2 mL
2¼ cups	vegetable stock	550 mL
	Salt and pepper	
1 cup	couscous	250 mL
¼ cup	chopped fresh coriander or parsley	50 mL
1	tomato, chopped	1

- Sort lentils, discarding any discolored ones. Rinse under cold water; drain and set aside.

- In saucepan, heat oil over medium-high heat; sauté onion, celery, red pepper, garlic, ginger, coriander and cumin for 5 minutes.

- Stir in lentils and 1⅔ cups (400 mL) of the stock; bring to boil. Reduce heat; cover and simmer, stirring occasionally, for 30 minutes or until lentils are tender. Season with salt and pepper to taste.

- Meanwhile, in saucepan, bring remaining stock to boil; stir in couscous. Cover and remove from heat; let stand for 5 minutes. Fluff with fork; stir in half of the fresh coriander, and salt and pepper to taste.

- To serve, spoon stew over couscous; sprinkle with tomato and remaining coriander.

Makes 4 servings.

PER SERVING: about 410 calories, 20 g protein, 5 g fat, 73 g carbohydrate, very high source fibre, excellent source iron.

Vegetarian Chili in Sweet Potato Boats

A pot of chili is always a crowd pleaser. For something different, try this black bean version with corn kernels served in a scooped-out baked sweet potato.

6	large sweet potatoes	6
1 tbsp	olive oil	15 mL
2	sweet green peppers, diced	2
2	onions, chopped	2
2	cloves garlic, minced	2
1 tbsp	chili powder	15 mL
2 tsp	ground cumin	10 mL
1 tsp	ground coriander	5 mL
	Salt and pepper	
1	can (28 oz/796 mL) tomatoes (undrained), chopped	1
1	can (14 oz/398 mL) black beans, drained and rinsed	1
1 cup	corn kernels	250 mL
¼ cup	chopped fresh coriander or parsley	50 mL
⅓ cup	plain yogurt	75 mL
	Fresh coriander leaves	
	Lime wedges	

• Pierce sweet potatoes all over with fork. Bake in 400°F (200°C) oven for about 1½ hours or until tender.

• Meanwhile, in large nonstick skillet, heat oil over medium heat; cook green peppers, onions, garlic, chili powder, cumin, coriander, ½ tsp (2 mL) salt and ¼ tsp (1 mL) pepper, stirring, for 10 minutes.

• Stir in tomatoes and black beans; bring to boil. Reduce heat, cover and simmer for 20 minutes. Stir in corn and 2 tbsp (25 mL) of the chopped coriander; cook, uncovered, for 5 minutes. Add remaining chopped coriander.

• Place sweet potatoes on plates; slit lengthwise through middle and mash inside slightly with fork. Season with salt and pepper to taste. Using back of spoon, make hollows in sweet potatoes; spoon in chili mixture. Top with spoonful of yogurt. Garnish with coriander leaves and lime.

Makes 6 servings.

PER SERVING: about 360 calories, 11 g protein, 4 g fat, 74 g carbohydrate, very high source fibre, excellent source iron.

Lean and Hearty Beef Stew

This lean stew has everything going for it — a good boost of iron and fibre, plus great full-bodied taste and a fuss-free preparation.

1 lb	mushrooms	500 g
2	large onions	2
2 tsp	vegetable oil	10 mL
1½ lb	lean stewing beef, cut in 2-inch (5 cm) cubes	750 g
¼ cup	all-purpose flour	50 mL
¼ tsp	each dried thyme, cumin and hot pepper flakes	1 mL
3 cups	beef stock	750 mL
1 tbsp	balsamic or red wine vinegar	15 mL
4	parsnips, peeled and chopped	4
6	carrots, chopped	6
3	potatoes, peeled and quartered	3
	Salt and pepper	

- Trim stems from mushrooms; chop stems and 1 of the onions.

- In Dutch oven, heat oil over medium-high heat; brown beef all over. Add mushroom stems and chopped onion; cover and cook over medium-low heat, stirring occasionally, for 5 minutes or until softened.

- Mix together flour, thyme, cumin and hot pepper flakes; whisk into stock and stir in vinegar. Add to pan and bring to simmer, stirring; cover and simmer for 40 minutes.

- Cut remaining onion into thin wedges. Add to pan along with parsnips, carrots, potatoes and mushroom caps; simmer, covered, for about 35 minutes or until vegetables are tender. Season with salt and pepper to taste.

Makes 6 servings.
PER SERVING: about 405 calories, 32 g protein, 8 g fat, 52 g carbohydrate, very high source fibre, excellent source iron.

Sauerbraten Beef Stew

Gingersnaps and vinegar give a sweet-and-sour tang to this stew, which, by the way, freezes well. It's excellent with mashed potatoes and a red cabbage salad.

4 tsp	vegetable oil	20 mL
2 lb	lean stewing beef (blade roast or chuck), cut in 1-inch (2.5 cm) cubes	1 kg
2	onions, chopped	2
2½ cups	beef stock or water	625 mL
½ cup	cider vinegar	125 mL
¼ cup	packed brown sugar	50 mL
2	bay leaves	2
¼ tsp	each salt and pepper	1 mL
Pinch	each allspice and ground cloves	Pinch
4	large carrots, thickly sliced	4
½ cup	crushed gingersnap cookies	125 mL
¼ cup	raisins	50 mL

- In Dutch oven, heat half of the oil over high heat; brown beef, in batches and adding remaining oil as needed. Transfer beef to plate and set aside.

- Pour off any fat in pan. Reduce heat to medium-low; cook onions, stirring occasionally, for 5 minutes or until softened. Return beef to pan; add stock, vinegar, sugar, bay leaves, salt, pepper, allspice and cloves. Bring to boil; reduce heat, cover and simmer for 1 hour.

- Add carrots; simmer, covered, for about 20 minutes or until tender. Add gingersnaps and raisins; simmer for 5 minutes or until thickened. Discard bay leaves.

Makes 6 servings.
PER SERVING: about 390 calories, 31 g protein, 15 g fat, 34 g carbohydrate, excellent source iron.

TIP: Brown meat in batches. Adding too much meat to the skillet at one time will cause meat to steam, not brown nicely.

Cabbage Vegetable Soup

Here's a soup that is so thick and chunky it's almost a stew! For a vegetarian version, use vegetable stock.

1 tbsp	vegetable oil	15 mL
1	onion, chopped	1
4	cloves garlic, chopped	4
2	large potatoes (unpeeled), cut in chunks	2
4	carrots, sliced	4
1	can (10 oz/284 mL) chicken stock	1
1¼ cups	water	300 mL
1	can (19 oz/540 mL) tomatoes (undrained), chopped	1
2 tbsp	chopped fresh dill (or 1 tbsp/ 15 mL dried dillweed)	25 mL
½ tsp	each caraway seeds, celery seeds and salt	2 mL
¼ tsp	each pepper and nutmeg	1 mL
4 cups	coarsely sliced trimmed cabbage	1 L
1 cup	shredded spinach (optional)	250 mL

- In large saucepan, heat oil over medium heat; cook onion and garlic, stirring occasionally, for 7 to 10 minutes or until softened.

- Add potatoes, carrots, chicken stock, water, tomatoes, half of the dill, the caraway seeds, celery seeds, salt, pepper and nutmeg; bring to boil. Reduce heat to medium; cover and simmer for 20 minutes.

- Add cabbage; cook for 25 minutes or until tender. Add spinach (if using); cook, uncovered, for 2 minutes or until wilted. Ladle into bowls; garnish with remaining dill.

Makes 6 servings.
Per serving: about 147 calories, 6 g protein, 3 g fat, 26 g carbohydrate, high source fibre.

Crockpot Lentil Soup

Just imagine coming home on a bone-chilling day to find that the kitchen elves have left a tasty supper simmering and ready to serve. Thank goodness for Crockpot magic. This nifty electric slow cooker is not the newest appliance on the market, but one that more and more busy households are discovering.

6 cups	vegetable stock	1.5 L
1½ cups	green lentils	375 mL
1	onion, chopped	1
5	carrots, finely chopped	5
4	cloves garlic, chopped	4
1	can (5½ oz/156 mL) tomato paste	1
2 tsp	each ground cumin and dried oregano	10 mL
½ tsp	salt	2 mL
¼ tsp	pepper	1 mL
1	strip lemon rind	1
4 cups	shredded fresh spinach (or half 300 g pkg frozen)	1 L
½ cup	chopped fresh parsley	125 mL
2 tbsp	lemon juice	25 mL

- In large 22-cup (4.5 L) Crockpot, combine vegetable stock, lentils, onion, carrots, garlic, tomato paste, cumin, oregano, salt, pepper and lemon rind. Cover and cook on high heat for 8 hours.
- Add spinach and parsley; cook for 30 to 60 minutes or until vegetables are tender. Stir in lemon juice.

Makes 4 servings.
PER SERVING: about 385 calories, 25 g protein, 3 g fat, 70 g carbohydrate, very high source fibre, good source calcium, excellent source iron.

CROCKPOT COOKING
- The Crockpot is designed to cook unattended, so do not peek; lifting the lid disrupts cooking.
- Because food cooks slowly, liquids reduce less and seasonings tend to be milder. So use slightly more seasoning and less liquid than in conventional cooking.

Cock-a-Leekie Soup

Ward off the shivers with a bowl of this Scottish chicken soup.

2 tbsp	vegetable oil	25 mL
2 cups	sliced leeks	500 mL
2	boneless skinless chicken breasts, cubed	2
6 cups	chicken stock (see Homemade Chicken Stock, page 38)	1.5 L
¾ cup	long-grain rice	175 mL
1	strip lemon rind	1
1	bay leaf	1
	Salt and pepper	
2 tbsp	chopped fresh parsley	25 mL

- In saucepan, heat oil over medium heat; cook leeks, covered, for 5 minutes or until softened. Add chicken; cook over medium-high heat, stirring, for 4 minutes.
- Stir in stock, rice, lemon rind and bay leaf; bring to boil. Reduce heat and simmer for about 20 minutes or until rice is tender. Discard lemon rind and bay leaf. Season with salt and pepper to taste. Ladle into bowls; garnish with parsley.

Makes 4 servings.
PER SERVING: about 320 calories, 24 g protein, 10 g fat, 31 g carbohydrate.

TIP: Don't let the lack of homemade chicken stock stand in the way of making chicken soup. Canned chicken broth, especially the low-sodium one, is a good substitute. If using regular canned broth, cubes or powder as a stock base, do not add salt during cooking time. Season to taste before serving.

Chicken Tortilla Soup

There's a Jewish chicken soup, Chinese chicken soup, Scottish chicken soup, Greek chicken soup and more. And just to show there's never enough of a good thing, here's one with a gentle Mexican twist.

3	boneless skinless chicken breasts	3
4	4-inch (10 cm) corn tortillas	4
2 tbsp	vegetable oil	25 mL
2	cloves garlic, minced	2
1	onion, chopped	1
1 tsp	ground cumin	5 mL
¼ tsp	chili powder	1 mL
1	each sweet red and yellow pepper, chopped	1
4	plum tomatoes, chopped	4
4 cups	chicken stock	1 L
1 cup	corn kernels	250 mL
1 tbsp	lime juice	15 mL
¼ cup	chopped fresh coriander	50 mL

- Cut chicken diagonally into ¼-inch (5 mm) thick strips; set aside. Cut tortillas into ¼-inch (5 mm) thick strips.

- In large saucepan, heat 1 tbsp (15 mL) of the oil over medium-high heat; cook tortilla strips, stirring, for about 2 minutes or until crisp. With slotted spoon, remove and drain on paper towels.

- Add remaining oil, garlic, onion, cumin and chili powder to pan; cook over medium heat, stirring occasionally, for 3 minutes or until softened.

- Add chicken and red and yellow peppers; cook for 5 minutes or until chicken is golden. Add tomatoes and chicken stock; bring to boil. Reduce heat and simmer for 7 minutes.

- Add corn; cook for 2 minutes. Stir in lime juice. Ladle into bowls; garnish with tortilla chips and coriander.

Makes 6 servings.
PER SERVING: about 210 calories, 20 g protein, 7 g fat, 18 g carbohydrate.

Turkey Barley Soup

Turn turkey bones and leftovers into a soul-warming and body-comforting soup.

1 cup	sliced carrots	250 mL
½ cup	sliced celery	125 mL
⅓ cup	pearl barley	75 mL
4 cups	cubed cooked turkey	1 L
½ cup	corn kernels	125 mL
	Salt and pepper	
2 tbsp	chopped fresh parsley	25 mL
BROTH:		
1	onion, chopped	1
2	carrots, chopped	2
1	bay leaf	1
10	peppercorns	10
¼ cup	parsley stalks	50 mL
1	turkey carcass	1
8 cups	water	2 L
1	can (10 oz/284 mL) chicken stock	1
1	can (19 oz/540 mL) tomatoes	1

- **BROTH:** In stockpot, combine onion, carrots, bay leaf, peppercorns, parsley, turkey carcass, water, chicken stock and tomatoes; bring to boil. Reduce heat and simmer for 2½ hours. Strain.

- In clean stockpot, combine strained turkey broth, carrots, celery and pearl barley; simmer for 30 minutes or until barley and vegetables are tender.

- Add turkey and corn; cook for 1 minute or until heated through. Season with salt and pepper to taste. Ladle into bowls; garnish with parsley.

Makes 6 servings.

PER SERVING: about 280 calories, 35 g protein, 7 g fat, 19 g carbohydrate, good source iron.

Black Bean and Bacon Soup

If beans can be called trendy, then the novelty, healthfulness and inky color of black beans rate them trendiest of all. Combined with bacon and a rainbow of vegetables, they simmer into something pretty special.

6	slices bacon, chopped	6
2	carrots, chopped	2
2	stalks celery, chopped	2
2	cloves garlic, minced	2
1	onion, chopped	1
1	sweet red pepper, chopped	1
2	cans (each 14 oz/398 mL) black beans, drained and rinsed	2
4 cups	chicken stock	1 L
1 tsp	dried sage	5 mL
1 tsp	red wine vinegar	5 mL
½ tsp	pepper	2 mL
¼ tsp	salt	1 mL

- In large saucepan or Dutch oven, cook bacon over high heat for about 5 minutes or until crisp. Drain off all but 1 tbsp (15 mL) fat from pan.

- Reduce heat to medium; cook carrots, celery, garlic, onion and red pepper for 5 minutes or until onion is softened.

- Add black beans, chicken stock and sage; bring to boil. Reduce heat, cover and simmer for 20 minutes or until vegetables are tender. Stir in vinegar, pepper and salt.

Makes 6 servings.

PER SERVING: about 230 calories, 14 g protein, 7 g fat, 29 g carbohydrate, very high source fibre, good source iron.

Rose Murray's Old-Fashioned Fish Chowder

Fish chowder is one of the simplest of all soups — wholesome fish, gently sautéed vegetables and a broth enriched with cream. Make it for a cosy supper with freshly baked biscuits and a salad.

2 lb	fresh or thawed haddock, halibut or cod fillets	1 kg
¼ lb	salt pork, diced (optional)	125 g
¼ cup	butter	50 mL
2	large onions, thinly sliced	2
2	small leeks, thinly sliced	2
½ cup	sliced celery	125 mL
4 cups	thinly sliced peeled potatoes (about 6 small)	1 L
1 tsp	dried thyme	5 mL
	Salt and pepper	
4 cups	boiling water	1 L
2 cups	milk	500 mL
2 cups	light cream	500 mL
2 tbsp	chopped fresh parsley or chives	25 mL
	Paprika	

- Remove any small bones from fish; cut into large bite-size pieces. Set aside.

- In large heavy pot, cook salt pork (if using) until crisp. Drain on paper towels; set aside. Drain off fat.

- In same pot, melt butter over low heat; cook onions, leeks and celery, stirring occasionally, for about 15 minutes or until softened but not browned. Stir in potatoes, thyme, and salt and pepper to taste; pour in boiling water and bring to boil.

- Reduce heat, cover and simmer for about 10 minutes or until potatoes are barely tender. Add fish; simmer, covered, for about 10 minutes or just until fish flakes easily when tested with fork.

- Stir in milk, cream, and fried pork (if using). Gently heat through but do not boil. Ladle into bowls; sprinkle with parsley and paprika.

Makes 8 servings.

PER SERVING: about 375 calories, 27 g protein, 19 g fat, 25 g carbohydrate, good source calcium.

Crusty Herbed Tortellini

Cosy up to this quick appealing casserole using store-bought tortellini.

1 tbsp	olive oil	15 mL
1	small onion, chopped	1
3	cloves garlic, minced	3
1½ cups	sliced mushrooms	375 mL
2 tbsp	chopped fresh basil (or 2 tsp/10 mL dried)	25 mL
1 tbsp	chopped fresh oregano (or 1 tsp/5 mL dried)	15 mL
½ tsp	each salt and pepper	2 mL
1	can (28 oz/796 mL) tomatoes	1
½ cup	milk	125 mL
3 tbsp	tomato paste	50 mL
1 lb	cheese-filled tortellini	500 g
¼ cup	chopped fresh parsley	50 mL
½ cup	shredded part-skim Danbo or Swiss cheese	125 mL
¼ cup	freshly grated Parmesan cheese	50 mL

- In large deep skillet or saucepan, heat oil over medium-high heat; cook onion and garlic, stirring occasionally, for 3 minutes or until softened. Add mushrooms, basil, oregano, salt and pepper; cook, stirring, for about 5 minutes or until moisture is evaporated.

- Meanwhile, in food processor, purée tomatoes; pour into skillet along with milk. Stir in tomato paste and bring to boil; reduce heat and simmer for 35 minutes or until thickened.

- In saucepan of boiling salted water, cook tortellini for about 8 minutes or until tender but firm. Drain well and add to sauce along with parsley.

- Pour into 10-cup (2.5 L) shallow casserole. Sprinkle with Danbo and Parmesan cheeses; broil for about 2 minutes or until cheese is melted and starting to turn golden.

Makes 4 servings.

PER SERVING: about 500 calories, 25 g protein, 15 g fat, 68 g carbohydrate, very high source fibre, excellent source calcium and iron.

Creamy Pearl Barley and Vegetable Risotto

At Capers Restaurant in Vancouver, barley often appears on the menu. Here's one of its most popular guises.

6 cups	vegetable or chicken stock	1.5 L
1½ cups	dry white wine or vegetable or chicken stock	375 mL
1¾ cups	pearl barley	425 mL
1 tbsp	olive oil	15 mL
2 cups	sliced mushrooms	500 mL
1	onion, chopped	1
1	clove garlic, minced	1
2 cups	diced peeled sweet potato	500 mL
1 tsp	dried thyme (or 1 tbsp/15 mL fresh)	5 mL
3 cups	small broccoli florets	750 mL
½ cup	freshly grated Parmesan cheese	125 mL
	Salt and pepper	

- Combine vegetable stock and white wine. In large heavy saucepan, combine 3½ cups (875 mL) of the stock mixture and barley; cover and bring to boil.

- Reduce heat to medium-low; simmer, covered, for 25 to 30 minutes or until almost all liquid is absorbed.

- Stir in 3 cups (750 mL) of the stock mixture, ½ cup (125 mL) at a time, stirring constantly until absorbed before next addition, for 25 minutes total or until barley is tender. Remove from heat; set aside.

- Meanwhile, in large saucepan, heat oil over medium heat; cook mushrooms, onion and garlic, stirring often, for 5 minutes or until mushrooms are soft.

- Stir in remaining stock, sweet potato and thyme; cover and simmer over medium-low heat for 8 minutes, stirring occasionally. Add broccoli; cook for 6 to 8 minutes or until vegetables are tender. Stir in barley; heat through, if necessary. Sprinkle with cheese, and salt and pepper to taste.

Makes 5 servings.

PER SERVING: about 440 calories, 13 g protein, 8 g fat, 78 g carbohydrate, very high source fibre, good source calcium, excellent source iron.

CHAPTER THREE

OUT OF THE OVEN

*The oven delivers its own
mealtime magic of crisp
toppings, caramelized golden
brown flavors and bubbly
fillings — all with as much
ease and as little tending as
long-simmering pots
atop the stove.*

Nicely Spiced Pork Loin

There's a hint of Morocco in the spices rubbed on the outside of this lean loin roast. As a side dish, carrots complement both the pork and the spices, as do green beans, sugar snap peas or broccoli.

4	cloves garlic, minced	4
1 tsp	salt	5 mL
2 tbsp	vegetable oil	25 mL
2 tbsp	lemon juice	25 mL
1 tbsp	paprika	15 mL
2 tsp	each ground cumin and coriander	10 mL
1 tsp	ginger	5 mL
¼ tsp	cinnamon	1 mL
1	boneless pork loin roast (about 4 lb/2 kg)	1

- In bowl, mash garlic with salt; mix in oil, lemon juice, paprika, cumin, coriander, ginger and cinnamon.

- Cut 1-inch (2.5 cm) deep slits all over top and sides of pork; rub paste all over roast. Roast on roasting rack in pan in 325°F (160°C) oven for about 1 hour and 45 minutes or until meat thermometer registers 160°F (70°C).

- Transfer to platter and tent with foil. Let stand for 10 minutes before carving.

Makes 8 servings.
Per serving: about 350 calories, 38 g protein, 20 g fat, 2 g carbohydrate, good source iron.

Asparagus Ham Strata

*Celebrate spring, asparagus and Mother's Day all at once with this savory baked bread, egg and cheese casserole.
It's just about perfect for a spring brunch, lunch or company supper.*

3½ cups	chopped asparagus (about 1½ lb/750 g)	875 mL
12	slices egg bread	12
½ lb	sliced cooked ham (about 6 slices)	250 g
1	sweet red pepper, chopped	1
1	onion, chopped	1
2 cups	shredded Swiss or mozzarella cheese	500 mL
2 cups	milk	500 mL
4	eggs	4
2 tbsp	Dijon mustard	25 mL
1 tsp	Worcestershire sauce	5 mL
¾ tsp	salt	4 mL
¼ tsp	pepper	1 mL
Pinch	cayenne pepper	Pinch

- In saucepan of boiling water, blanch asparagus for 2 minutes; drain and refresh under cold water. Reserve ½ cup (125 mL) tips for garnish.

- Trim crusts from bread; cut in half diagonally. Arrange 8 triangles on bottom of 13- x 9-inch (3 L) baking dish or 10-cup (2.5 L) oval casserole. Cut ham into 24 same-size triangles; arrange 8 triangles over bread. Sprinkle with all but ½ cup (125 mL) each of the red pepper and asparagus. Top with onion and half of the cheese.

- Lay remaining ham triangles over remaining bread triangles; arrange, overlapping slightly, around border of casserole, ham side up. Sprinkle remaining red pepper and asparagus in centre. Sprinkle with remaining cheese.

- Whisk together milk, eggs, mustard, Worcestershire sauce, salt, pepper and cayenne; pour evenly over strata. *(Strata can be prepared to this point, covered and refrigerated for up to 8 hours.)*

- Bake in 350°F (180°C) oven for 45 to 50 minutes or until set and golden, covering with foil to prevent bread from darkening too much. Let stand on rack for 10 minutes. Garnish with reserved asparagus tips.

Makes 8 servings.

Per serving: about 330 calories, 23 g protein, 17 g fat, 21 g carbohydrate, excellent source calcium, good source iron.

Orange Fennel Pork Roast Dinner

Pork is such a delicious answer to affordable and stylish entertaining. If you have never tried fennel, here it is in seed form, sharing its mildly licorice taste with ginger, orange and garlic for an unusual and very appealing flavor combo.

1	loin rack of pork, rib end (4 lb/2 kg)	1
3	cloves garlic, slivered	3
2 tbsp	minced gingerroot	25 mL
4 tsp	fennel seeds, crushed	20 mL
½ tsp	salt	2 mL
¼ tsp	pepper	1 mL
	Roast Vegetables (recipe below)	
GLAZE:		
½ cup	frozen orange juice concentrate	125 mL
½ cup	water	125 mL
¼ cup	orange marmalade	50 mL
2 tsp	grated orange rind	10 mL
2 tsp	cornstarch	10 mL

- Cut tiny slits all over pork; insert garlic slivers. Combine ginger, fennel seeds, salt and pepper; rub over pork. Wrap ends of ribs in foil to prevent charring. Place, rib ends up, on rack in shallow roasting pan. Roast in 325°F (160°C) oven for 30 minutes.

- GLAZE: Meanwhile, in small saucepan, cook orange juice concentrate, water, marmalade, orange rind and cornstarch over medium-high heat, whisking constantly, for 3 to 5 minutes or until boiling and thickened. Remove ½ cup (125 mL) for basting; set remaining glaze aside.

- Brush pork with some of the basting glaze. Roast, basting every 20 minutes, for 2 to 2¼ hours longer or until meat thermometer registers 160° to 170°F (70° to 75°C). Transfer to platter; tent with foil and let stand for 15 minutes.

- Rewarm reserved glaze over low heat; spoon over meat. Surround meat with Roast Vegetables.

Makes 8 servings.
PER SERVING (without roast vegetable): about 295 calories, 31 g protein, 15 g fat, 8 g carbohydrate.

Roast Vegetables

Roasting vegetables used to be confined to times when a standing rib roast was on the menu. You don't have to wait until then, though, to enjoy the crispy golden edges and concentrated tastes vegetables deliver via the oven.

5	potatoes	5
4	onions	4
1	bunch celery	1
1	acorn squash	1
⅓ cup	vegetable oil	75 mL
¾ tsp	salt	4 mL
¼ tsp	pepper	1 mL

- Peel and quarter potatoes and onions. Cut bunch of celery 3 inches (8 cm) from base, reserving stalks for other use. Cut base into thick wedges, leaving stem end intact. Cut squash in half; seed and cut into wedges.

- In large bowl, combine oil, salt and pepper; add potatoes, onions, celery and squash and toss to coat. Place on greased baking sheet; bake in 325°F (160°C) oven for 1½ hours, rearranging occasionally. Broil for 5 minutes or until lightly browned.

Makes 8 servings.
PER SERVING: about 200 calories, 3 g protein, 9 g fat, 29 g carbohydrate.

Gratin of Creamed Spinach and Eggs

This is one versatile little casserole. With hard-cooked eggs and ham, it's a brilliant and inexpensive way to use up Easter weekend leftovers.

3 tbsp	butter	50 mL
1 cup	fresh bread crumbs	250 mL
1	onion, sliced	1
¼ cup	all-purpose flour	50 mL
2 cups	1% milk	500 mL
½ tsp	each salt (approx) and nutmeg	2 mL
¼ tsp	pepper	1 mL
1	pkg (10 oz/300 g) frozen chopped spinach, thawed and squeezed dry	1
½ cup	freshly grated Parmesan cheese	125 mL
6	hard-cooked eggs	6
1 cup	thin strips ham (optional)	250 mL

- In large saucepan, melt butter; remove 1 tbsp (15 mL) and toss with bread crumbs. Set aside.

- Add onion to pan; cook over low heat, stirring often, for 5 minutes or until softened. Sprinkle with flour; cook, stirring, for 1 minute. Gradually whisk in milk, salt, nutmeg and pepper; cook, stirring, over medium heat for about 3 minutes or until thickened. Add spinach and Parmesan cheese; cook for 1 minute.

- Quarter eggs lengthwise; place, cut side up, in greased 6-cup (1.5 L) baking dish. Sprinkle with salt to taste. Arrange ham (if using) over eggs. Spread spinach mixture evenly over top; sprinkle with bread crumbs. Bake in 375°F (190°C) oven for 20 minutes or until browned.

Makes 4 servings.

Per serving: about 385 calories, 22 g protein, 22 g fat, 24 g carbohydrate, excellent source calcium, good source iron.

Zurich Beans

The lips of the community of Zurich, Ontario, are sealed concerning the fabulous secret recipe they dish out to visitors at their annual bean festival. Journalist Wayne Kelly supplied the following recipe with the assurance that it is tantalizingly close.

2½ cups	white pea beans	625 mL
¼ lb	slab bacon, cubed	125 g
1½ cups	tomato juice	375 mL
1 cup	packed brown sugar	250 mL
1 cup	ketchup	250 mL
1 tbsp	salt	15 mL
½ tsp	dry mustard	2 mL
½ tsp	pepper	2 mL

- In large saucepan, pour 8 cups (2 L) water over beans; bring to boil and boil for 2 minutes. Remove from heat; let stand for 1 hour. Drain, discarding liquid.

- In same saucepan, pour 8 cups (2 L) fresh water over beans; bring to boil. Reduce heat, cover and simmer for 30 to 45 minutes or until beans are tender. Drain, reserving liquid.

- In casserole, combine beans, bacon, tomato juice, sugar, ketchup, salt, mustard and pepper. Cover and bake in 300°F (150°C) oven for 3 to 3½ hours or until tender, checking every 45 minutes and stirring in reserved liquid, if necessary, to moisten beans.

Makes 6 servings.

Per serving: about 580 calories, 20 g protein, 12 g fat, 102 g carbohydrate, very high source fibre, good source calcium, excellent source iron.

Texas Steak "Pot Roast"

This delicious little version of a pot roast is just right for four.
There's plenty of sauce for creamy mashed potatoes on the side.

1 tbsp	olive oil	15 mL
1¼ lb	outside round steak, trimmed	625 g
	Salt and pepper	
1 cup	beef stock	250 mL
1 cup	bottled salsa	250 mL
2 tbsp	lime juice	25 mL
2	onions, sliced	2
2	cloves garlic, minced	2
2 tsp	ground cumin	10 mL
¼ tsp	hot pepper flakes	1 mL

- In Dutch oven or deep ovenproof skillet, heat oil over medium heat; brown steak all over. Sprinkle with salt and pepper. Transfer to plate and set aside.

- Stir stock into pan; bring to boil, stirring to scrape up brown bits. Stir in salsa, lime juice, onions, garlic, cumin and hot pepper flakes; bring to boil.

- Return meat to pan. Cover tightly; bake in 325°F (160°C) oven, turning meat every 30 minutes, for 2 to 2½ hours or until very tender.

- *(Pot roast can be cooled in refrigerator, covered and stored for up to 12 hours. Or freeze for up to 2 months; thaw in refrigerator, then bring to room temperature. Reheat in 350°F/180°C oven for about 30 minutes or until heated through.)* Slice steak thinly and spoon sauce over top.

Makes 4 servings.
PER SERVING: about 280 calories, 34 g protein, 11 g fat, 10 g carbohydrate, excellent source iron.

THE SKINNY ON POTATOES

START WITH MASHED: The low-down on mashed potatoes is that they're better moistened with low-fat buttermilk (by the way, all buttermilk sold in Canada is low-fat, from skim to 2%) than with a load of cream and butter. Try these for a four-person household.

Peel and quarter 4 large potatoes (about 1 lb/500 g). Yukon Gold potatoes are ideal because of their rich buttery color, but most other mature potatoes taste good, too. Cook in lightly salted boiling water in covered saucepan until tender, about 20 minutes. Drain and return to heat to dry for about 30 seconds. Mash with potato masher until smooth, or press through ricer. Mash with about ¾ cup (175 mL) buttermilk. Season with ground pepper. Reckon on about 200 calories and less than a gram of fat per satisfying serving. Of course, if you don't have buttermilk, low-fat milk will do, but it doesn't add the same fresh dairy taste as buttermilk.

ADD TASTE SENSATIONS: Treat potatoes like a foundation for building flavors with fresh herbs. Parsley, of course, the flat-leaf Italian, has the most taste, but chives and chervil can also be added in quantity. Fresh dill, basil, thyme, oregano, marjoram and tarragon should be stirred in with a scant hand. Roasted or braised garlic (see page 61) is good on its own, or with feta cheese melted in, and can make mashed potatoes into an entrée for a vegetarian in the family. Lightly sautéed onions, slivered sweet peppers or sun-dried tomatoes are truly sensational additions to plain mashed potatoes. Don't forget, you can cook other root vegetables such as carrots, parsnips and rutabaga with the potatoes, mash them and count on two vegetables at once.

ENJOY THEM BAKED: For small households, try the microwave. To prepare, prick potatoes in several places; place around the edge of microwaveable plate or turntable, calculating about 4 minutes for the first, and adding 2 minutes per extra spud.

While the microwave is fast, the dry heat of the oven does deliver crisp-skinned, fluffy-fleshed baked potatoes. Scrub and prick potatoes; bake in 400°F (200°C) oven for about 45 minutes or until potatoes yield to gentle squeeze. Sweet potatoes, with a tally of calories less than 150 and only a trace of fat per tuber — similar to white potatoes in both respects — can be prepared in the same way.

Oven-Barbecued Brisket

The aroma of this easy-to-put-together and even-easier-to-tend brisket will have helpers rushing to the kitchen to mash the potatoes and cook the carrot and broccoli side dishes.

6	onions	6
4	cloves garlic, chopped	4
1 tbsp	vegetable oil	15 mL
1	beef brisket (5 to 6 lb/2.2 to 3 kg)	1
1 tsp	each salt, pepper and paprika	5 mL
2 cups	beef stock	500 mL
⅔ cup	each ketchup and red wine vinegar	150 mL
3 tbsp	packed brown sugar	50 mL
2 tbsp	each Worcestershire sauce and soy sauce	25 mL
1 tsp	mustard	5 mL
½ tsp	hot pepper sauce	2 mL

- Slice onions thinly; separate into rings. Toss with garlic and oil; arrange over bottom of roasting pan. Top with brisket, fat side up; rub salt, pepper and paprika over top of meat.

- Combine beef stock, ketchup, vinegar, sugar, Worcestershire sauce, soy sauce, mustard and hot pepper sauce; pour over meat. Cover and bake in 325°F (160°C) oven, turning over halfway through, for 3½ to 4 hours or until meat is very tender.

- Transfer meat to serving platter and tent with foil; let stand for 10 minutes. Skim fat from sauce. Slice meat thinly and serve with sauce in sauceboat.

Makes 8 servings.

PER SERVING: about 470 calories, 46 g protein, 21 g fat, 24 g carbohydrate, excellent source iron.

Honey Lemon Roasted Chicken

Canada produces the world's best honey in an incredible number of flavors, depending on the blossoms the bees visit. Here, one of our milder honeys, such as alfalfa or canola, meets up with lemon to glaze an old-fashioned family favorite.

1	large lemon	1
1	roaster chicken (about 4 lb/2 kg)	1
	Pepper	
SAUCE:		
½ cup	liquid honey	125 mL
1 tbsp	chopped fresh basil (or 1 tsp/5 mL dried)	15 mL
½ tsp	each salt and pepper	2 mL

- Grate rind of lemon to make 2 tsp (10 mL); halve lemon and squeeze to make ¼ cup (50 mL) juice. Reserve rind, juice and lemon shells.

- Remove giblets and neck from chicken. Rinse and pat chicken dry inside and out; place lemon shells in cavity. Sprinkle chicken lightly with pepper. Tie legs together with string; tuck wings under back. Place, breast side up, on greased rack in roasting pan. Roast in 325°F (160°C) oven, basting occasionally, for 1¾ hours.

- SAUCE: Stir together honey and reserved lemon juice; brush 2 tbsp (25 mL) over chicken. Set remaining honey mixture aside.

- Roast chicken for about 20 minutes longer or until juices run clear when thigh is pierced and meat thermometer registers 185°F (85°C). Transfer to platter; tent with foil and let stand for 10 minutes.

- Meanwhile, skim fat from pan juices; whisk in reserved honey mixture, lemon rind, basil, salt and pepper. Bring to boil; boil, stirring occasionally, for 5 minutes or until thickened slightly. Serve with chicken.

Makes 4 servings.
PER SERVING: about 520 calories, 54 g protein, 17 g fat, 36 g carbohydrate, good source iron.

TIPS
- For more flavor in the Honey Lemon Roasted Chicken, gently separate some of the skin from the breast and tuck thin slices of lemon in between before roasting.
- To calculate roasting time of a different-size chicken, roast for 20 to 30 minutes per pound (500 g).

Citrusy Garlic Chicken

Garlic lovers, here you go! This recipe helps you appreciate the mellow richness of slow-baked garlic.

2	whole heads garlic	2
4	chicken legs, skinned	4
2 tsp	grated orange rind	10 mL
¼ cup	orange juice	50 mL
1 tbsp	chopped fresh basil (or 1 tsp/5 mL dried)	15 mL
1 tsp	olive oil	5 mL
½ tsp	pepper	2 mL
¼ tsp	salt	1 mL

- Separate garlic heads into cloves and peel; arrange in 8-inch (2 L) square baking dish. Place chicken over top.

- Stir together orange rind and juice, basil, oil, pepper and salt; pour over chicken. Cover and bake in 325°F (160°C) oven, basting once, for 1 hour or until juices run clear when chicken is pierced.

- Pour pan juices and garlic into food processor or blender; purée until smooth. Broil chicken for 3 to 5 minutes or until well browned on top. Serve with sauce.

Makes 4 servings.
PER SERVING: about 190 calories, 27 g protein, 6 g fat, 6 g carbohydrate.

Golden Garlic Chicken with Sweet Potatoes

Roasted chicken legs and breasts make an easy family or company dinner. Mellow baked garlic adds a new touch to this old favorite, as do nutritious sweet potatoes.

3	chicken legs	3
3	chicken breasts	3
3	sweet potatoes	3
3 tbsp	lemon juice	50 mL
2 tbsp	vegetable oil	25 mL
1 tbsp	crumbled dried rosemary (or 3 tbsp/50 mL fresh)	15 mL
1 tsp	each salt and pepper	5 mL
4	whole heads garlic (unpeeled)	4
1 tsp	olive oil	5 mL
	Fresh rosemary sprigs	

ROASTED GARLIC

To roast whole heads of garlic on their own, pull off papery outer layer. Cut off tips to expose the garlic. Place in pan, drizzle lightly with olive oil and sprinkle with herbs. Roast, covered, in 350°F (180°C) oven or toaster oven for about 45 minutes or until tender and golden. Squeeze out into mashed potatoes, pop into pasta sauces or serve a whole head per person, with toasted slices of crusty bread.

- Trim chicken and cut into pieces, severing legs at joint and cutting breasts in half crosswise. Peel potatoes; cut into ¼-inch (5 mm) thick slices.

- In bowl, toss together potatoes, chicken, lemon juice, vegetable oil, rosemary, salt and pepper. Arrange potatoes in single layer in 13- x 9-inch (3 L) baking dish. Top with chicken, skin side up. Cover and marinate in refrigerator for 4 hours.

- Trim tops from garlic heads; brush with olive oil and wrap in foil. Nestle into chicken and potatoes.

- Roast in 425°F (220°C) oven, basting occasionally, for 30 minutes. Remove garlic and discard foil; return garlic to pan. Roast, basting a few times, for 30 to 45 minutes or until juices run clear when chicken is pierced. Serve garnished with rosemary sprigs.

Makes 8 servings.
PER SERVING: about 310 calories, 24 g protein, 15 g fat, 18 g carbohydrate.

Baked Halibut with Stewed Tomatoes

Writer Anita Stewart adapted this recipe from a family favorite of Brenda Humchitt of the West Coast Heiltsuk Band.

2 tbsp	butter	25 mL
2	onions, sliced	2
1½ cups	canned plum tomatoes (including juice)	375 mL
½ tsp	each salt and pepper	2 mL
1½ lb	halibut steaks	750 g
1 tbsp	chopped fresh basil (or 1 tsp/5 mL dried)	15 mL

- In heavy saucepan, melt butter over medium heat; cook onions, stirring occasionally, for about 10 minutes or just until beginning to brown. Stir in tomatoes, breaking up with fork. Sprinkle with half of the salt and pepper; cook for about 3 minutes or until slightly thickened.

- Meanwhile, cut halibut into 6 or 8 pieces; remove bones. Sprinkle with remaining salt and pepper; place in greased 13- x 9-inch (3 L) baking dish. Spoon tomato sauce over top; sprinkle with basil. Bake in 450°F (230°C) oven for 10 to 15 minutes or until fish flakes easily when tested with fork.

Makes 6 servings.

PER SERVING: about 235 calories, 14 g protein, 17 g fat, 6 g carbohydrate.

Hearty Tuna Casserole

Rotini pasta, thin slices of zucchini and tomatoes update a cosy supper favorite from Lise LaPointe of Coaticook, Quebec, who contributed this recipe to Canadian Living's *special anniversary issue.*

3 cups	rotini pasta	750 mL
2	cans (each 6½ oz/184 g) chunk-style tuna, drained	2
½ cup	chopped celery	125 mL
2	green onions, sliced	2
⅔ cup	light sour cream	150 mL
½ cup	light mayonnaise	125 mL
2 tsp	Dijon mustard	10 mL
½ tsp	dried thyme	2 mL
½ tsp	salt	2 mL
¼ tsp	pepper	1 mL
1	small zucchini, thinly sliced	1
1	tomato, sliced	1
1 cup	shredded Monterey Jack cheese	250 mL

- In large pot of boiling salted water, cook rotini for about 8 minutes or until tender but firm; drain and rinse.

- In large bowl, flake tuna; add pasta, celery and onions. Stir in sour cream, mayonnaise, mustard, thyme, salt and pepper; spoon half into greased 8-cup (2 L) casserole.

- Layer zucchini over top; spread with remaining tuna mixture. Arrange tomato over top; sprinkle with cheese. Bake in 350°F (180°C) oven for 30 minutes or until hot and bubbly.

Makes 4 servings.

PER SERVING: about 550 calories, 37 g protein, 27 g fat, 39 g carbohydrate, excellent source calcium, good source iron.

Bonnie Stern's Sesame Salmon

Toronto cooking school owner, author and food writer Bonnie Stern takes a new light approach to cooking for this satisfying warm salad.

8 cups	mixed salad greens	2 L
SESAME SALMON:		
4	salmon fillets (each 4 oz/125 g), skinned	4
1 tbsp	liquid honey	15 mL
1 tsp	soy sauce	5 mL
1 tsp	sweet mustard	5 mL
2 tbsp	sesame seeds	25 mL
1 tsp	olive oil	5 mL
ORIENTAL DRESSING:		
3 tbsp	orange juice	50 mL
2 tbsp	soy sauce	25 mL
2 tbsp	rice vinegar or balsamic vinegar	25 mL
1 tbsp	sesame oil	15 mL
2 tsp	liquid honey	10 mL
2 tsp	sweet mustard	10 mL
1	clove garlic, minced	1
1 tsp	minced gingerroot	5 mL
¼ tsp	hot pepper sauce (optional)	1 mL

- SESAME SALMON: Pat salmon dry. Pull out any small bones. Combine honey, soy sauce and mustard; brush over salmon. Sprinkle with sesame seeds. In nonstick skillet, heat oil over high heat; cook salmon for 30 seconds on each side.

- Transfer to rimmed baking sheet if skillet is not ovenproof. Bake in 425°F (220°C) oven for 7 to 8 minutes or just until fish flakes easily when tested with fork.

- ORIENTAL DRESSING: Meanwhile, in small bowl, whisk together orange juice, soy sauce, vinegar, oil, honey, mustard, garlic, ginger, and hot pepper sauce (if using); pour over salad greens in bowl and toss to coat. Divide among plates; top each with salmon.

Makes 4 servings.
PER SERVING: about 330 calories, 28 g protein, 18 g fat, 16 g carbohydrate, good source iron.

Biscuit-Topped Turkey Pot Pie

This update of a comforting old-fashioned standby uses convenient prepared dough so you don't have to make the biscuits from scratch.

1 tbsp	butter	15 mL
1	small onion, chopped	1
1	large potato, peeled and cut in bite-size cubes	1
1 lb	turkey or chicken breast, cubed (about 2½ cups/625 mL)	500 g
2	stalks celery, chopped	2
2	carrots, chopped	2
Half	sweet red pepper, chopped	Half
2½ cups	quartered mushrooms	625 mL
1 tsp	dried thyme	5 mL
½ tsp	salt	2 mL
¼ tsp	pepper	1 mL
¼ cup	all-purpose flour	50 mL
1⅔ cups	chicken stock	400 mL
1	pkg (212 g) buttermilk biscuit dough	1

- In large nonstick skillet, melt butter over medium-high heat; cook onion, potato, turkey, celery and carrots, stirring often, for 8 minutes. Stir in red pepper, mushrooms, thyme, salt and pepper; cook, stirring, for about 5 minutes or until turkey is no longer pink inside and vegetables are tender-crisp.

- Sprinkle with flour, stirring well; stir in stock and bring to boil, stirring constantly. Reduce heat and simmer for 1 minute or until thickened. Pour into 8-cup (2 L) casserole dish.

- Separate biscuit dough at perforations; arrange, with sides touching, over turkey mixture. Bake in 400°F (200°C) oven for 20 to 25 minutes or until biscuit tops are golden and undersides are firm, shielding with foil partway through if necessary to prevent overbrowning.

Makes 4 servings.

PER SERVING: about 430 calories, 36 g protein, 9 g fat, 49 g carbohydrate, high source fibre, excellent source iron.

Lasagna Meat Loaf

Some people joke about meat loaf. Perhaps they think meat loaf is some careless concoction budget-minded cooks throw in the oven to keep the hungry wolves at bay. But not this one. Smartened up with a three-cheese filling and a basil tomato sauce, its lasagna touches make it fancy enough for special occasions.

6 cups	fresh spinach	1.5 L
1	egg	1
1 cup	ricotta cheese	250 mL
½ cup	shredded part-skim mozzarella cheese	125 mL
2 tbsp	freshly grated Parmesan cheese	25 mL
2 tbsp	chopped fresh parsley	25 mL
2 tbsp	milk	25 mL
¼ tsp	each salt and pepper	1 mL
Pinch	nutmeg	Pinch

MEAT LAYER:

1	egg	1
1	onion, chopped	1
2	cloves garlic, minced	2
½ cup	dry bread crumbs	125 mL
2 tbsp	freshly grated Parmesan cheese	25 mL
1 tsp	each dried basil and oregano	5 mL
¾ tsp	salt	4 mL
½ tsp	pepper	2 mL
1½ lb	lean ground beef	750 g

SAUCE:

1 tbsp	vegetable oil	15 mL
1	onion, chopped	1
2	cloves garlic, minced	2
1 tsp	dried basil	5 mL
2	cans (each 19 oz/540 mL) tomatoes (undrained), chopped	2
1	can (5½ oz/156 mL) tomato paste	1
	Salt and pepper	

- SAUCE: In skillet, heat oil over medium heat; cook onion, garlic and basil, stirring occasionally, for 3 minutes. Stir in tomatoes and ½ cup (125 mL) of the tomato paste; bring to boil. Reduce heat and simmer, stirring often, for 20 minutes or until thickened. Season with salt and pepper to taste.

- Trim spinach and rinse under water; shake off excess water. In saucepan, cook spinach, covered, with just the water clinging to leaves, over medium-high heat for 2 to 3 minutes or just until wilted. Drain and set aside.

- Combine egg, ricotta, mozzarella and Parmesan cheeses, parsley, milk, salt, pepper and nutmeg; set aside.

- MEAT LAYER: In bowl, beat egg; mix in remaining tomato paste, onion, garlic, bread crumbs, Parmesan cheese, basil, oregano, salt and pepper. Mix in meat. Place between sheets of waxed paper; roll into 18- x 8-inch (45 x 20 cm) rectangle. Remove top sheet.

- Layer spinach leaves over meat. Gently spread ricotta mixture over spinach, leaving 1-inch (2.5 cm) border. Spread 1 cup (250 mL) of the sauce over ricotta layer. Roll up meat from short end, jelly roll style, lifting with paper and tucking in any filling that oozes out.

- Ease, seam side up, into 9- x 5-inch (2 L) loaf pan. Bake in 350°F (180°C) oven for 1 to 1¼ hours or until meat is no longer pink. Let stand for 20 minutes. Drain off fat. Heat remaining sauce and serve with loaf.

Makes 8 servings.
PER SERVING: about 370 calories, 29 g protein, 19 g fat, 21 g carbohydrate, high source fibre, excellent source calcium and iron.

Three-Cheese Baked Penne with Roasted Vegetables

This is a pretty fancy version of mac and cheese, but once you've tasted it, you'll know that roasting the vegetables and blending the cheeses was more than worth the effort.

1	each sweet red and yellow pepper, chopped	1
3 cups	quartered mushrooms (½ lb/250 g)	750 mL
2	zucchini, diced	2
1	small eggplant, diced	1
3	cloves garlic, minced	3
¼ cup	olive oil	50 mL
	Salt and pepper	
½ cup	chopped fresh parsley	125 mL
2 tbsp	chopped fresh basil (or 2 tsp/10 mL dried)	25 mL
½ tsp	dried rosemary	2 mL
5 cups	penne pasta	1.25 L
1	can (28 oz/796 mL) meatless spaghetti sauce	1
3½ cups	shredded mozzarella cheese	875 mL
2 cups	diced Fontina cheese	500 mL
1 cup	freshly grated Parmesan cheese	250 mL

- In large shallow pan, toss together red and yellow peppers, mushrooms, zucchini, eggplant, garlic and oil; spread onto rimmed baking sheet. Bake in 500°F (260°C) oven, stirring once or twice, for about 20 minutes or until softened.

- Transfer to greased 13- x 9-inch (3 L) baking dish. Season with salt and pepper to taste. Stir in ⅓ cup (75 mL) of the parsley, basil and rosemary.

- Meanwhile, in large pot of boiling salted water, cook pasta for 8 to 10 minutes or until tender but firm. Drain well and rinse under cold water; let cool. Add to baking dish along with spaghetti sauce, mozzarella cheese, Fontina cheese and half of the Parmesan; toss to combine.

- Sprinkle with remaining Parmesan and parsley. *(Penne can be prepared to this point, covered and refrigerated for up to 1 day; bring to room temperature.)* Bake in 375°F (190°C) oven for 35 to 40 minutes or until bubbly.

Makes 8 servings.

PER SERVING: about 675 calories, 29 g protein, 33 g fat, 68 g carbohydrate, very high source fibre, excellent source calcium, good source iron.

Baked Mini Pumpkins

Charming little pumpkins make great fall table decorations and are equally significant as a vegetable side dish, here with a real Canadian splash of maple syrup.

4	mini pumpkins (about 8 oz/250 g each)	4
4 tsp	butter	20 mL
4 tsp	maple syrup	20 mL
4 tsp	chopped toasted pecans	20 mL
	Cinnamon	

- Cut off pumpkin tops; set aside. Scoop out seeds and stringy portions; discard. Divide butter and maple syrup among cavities; replace tops.

- In shallow baking dish, bake pumpkins in 375°F (190°C) oven for 35 to 45 minutes or until tender but still hold their shape. (Or microwave at High for 8 to 12 minutes, rotating once.)

- Sprinkle cavities evenly with pecans, and cinnamon to taste. Replace tops.

Makes 4 servings.
Per serving: about 110 calories, 2 g protein, 6 g fat, 15 g carbohydrate.

Sage-Roasted Mini New Potatoes

Burnished with paprika and crisped in the oven, tiny new potatoes become sweet and flavorful. For older large potatoes, simply cut, peeling only if absolutely necessary.

16	new potatoes (about 1 inch/2.5 cm)	16
2 tbsp	olive oil	25 mL
1 tbsp	minced fresh sage	15 mL
½ tsp	each coarse pepper and paprika	2 mL
¼ tsp	salt	1 mL
12	sprigs fresh sage	12

- Scrub and dry potatoes; do not peel. Place in shallow dish just large enough to arrange in single layer.

- Add oil, minced sage, pepper, paprika and salt; toss to coat well. Rearrange in single layer; tuck sage sprigs among potatoes.

- Roast, stirring once, in 350°F (180°C) oven for 45 to 60 minutes or until tender and skins are crisp.

Makes 4 servings.
Per serving: about 205 calories, 3 g protein, 7 g fat, 33 g carbohydrate.

Vegetarian Moussaka

Chunky eggplant gives substance to this robust mushroom-rich casserole. Serve as you would a lasagna — with a crisp green salad and crusty bread.

2	eggplants (2 lb/1 kg total)	2
¼ cup	freshly grated Parmesan cheese	50 mL

MUSHROOM FILLING:

1 tbsp	vegetable oil	15 mL
1	onion, chopped	1
3	cloves garlic, minced	3
½ tsp	each cinnamon, salt and pepper	2 mL
12 cups	sliced mushrooms (about 2 lb/1 kg)	3 L
¼ cup	dry red wine or mirin	50 mL
1	can (5½ oz/156 mL) tomato paste	1
½ cup	freshly grated Parmesan cheese	125 mL
½ cup	dry bread crumbs	125 mL
¼ cup	chopped fresh basil (or 4 tsp/20 mL dried)	50 mL

WHITE SAUCE:

¼ cup	vegetable oil or butter	50 mL
¼ cup	all-purpose flour	50 mL
1¼ cups	milk or soy milk	300 mL
¼ tsp	each salt and pepper	1 mL

- Peel and cut eggplants into ¼-inch (5 mm) thick slices. Arrange in single layer on lightly greased baking sheets; bake in 350°F (180°C) oven for 25 minutes. Let cool.

- MUSHROOM FILLING: Meanwhile, in Dutch oven, heat oil over medium heat; cook onion, garlic, cinnamon, salt and pepper, stirring occasionally, for 5 to 7 minutes or until softened.

- Stir in mushrooms and wine; cook for 10 minutes or until softened. Stir in tomato paste, Parmesan cheese, bread crumbs and basil; cover and simmer for 5 minutes or until most of the liquid is absorbed.

- WHITE SAUCE: Meanwhile, in large saucepan, heat oil over medium heat; whisk in flour and cook, stirring, for 1 minute. Gradually whisk in milk; cook, whisking, for 5 minutes or until thickened. Season with salt and pepper.

- Layer eggplant in greased 13- x 9-inch (3 L) baking dish, overlapping as necessary. Spread with mushroom filling, then white sauce. Sprinkle Parmesan cheese over top.

- Cover and bake in 350°F (180°C) oven for 20 minutes; uncover and bake for 10 minutes. Broil for 1 minute or until golden.

Makes 6 servings.

PER SERVING: about 345 calories, 14 g protein, 18 g fat, 36 g carbohydrate, very high source fibre, excellent source calcium and iron.

CHAPTER FOUR

A HEAD START

When time is short, you can relax knowing you have fabulous make-ahead dishes stowed in the refrigerator or freezer. Or maybe there's something marinating from earlier on, ready for a bit of last-minute attention, then enjoyment.

Tandoori Salmon

Appealing Indian flavors are in the yogurt mixture that both marinates the fish and turns into a golden baked-on coating.

4	salmon fillets (with skin) (4 oz/125 g each)	4
½ cup	plain yogurt	125 mL
1 tbsp	chopped fresh coriander or parsley	15 mL
1 tbsp	lemon juice	15 mL
1	clove garlic, minced	1
2 tsp	minced gingerroot	10 mL
1 tsp	ground cumin	5 mL
¾ tsp	paprika	4 mL
½ tsp	turmeric	2 mL
Pinch	each salt and pepper	Pinch

- Place salmon fillets, skin side down, in shallow glass dish. Pull out any small bones. Whisk together yogurt, coriander, lemon juice, garlic, ginger, cumin, paprika, turmeric, salt and pepper; pour over salmon. Cover and marinate in refrigerator for at least 4 hours or up to 24 hours.

- Shaking off excess marinade and reserving, place salmon, skin side up, on greased grill over medium-high heat; cook for 5 minutes. Turn and baste with marinade; cook for 4 to 6 minutes or until fish flakes easily when tested with fork.

Makes 4 servings.
PER SERVING: about 175 calories, 22 g protein, 7 g fat, 3 g carbohydrate.

Herb-Grilled Fish

Get a head start on a summer weekend dinner with this fresh herb marinade. Although there is oil in the marinade, much of it is lost during grilling.

¼ cup	vegetable oil	50 mL
2 tbsp	lemon juice	25 mL
1 tbsp	each minced fresh chives and parsley	15 mL
2 tsp	minced fresh thyme	10 mL
1	sprig fresh rosemary	1
1	clove garlic, minced	1
4	fish fillets or steaks, at least ¾ inch (2 cm) thick	4
	Salt and pepper	

- In shallow glass dish, combine oil, lemon juice, chives, parsley, thyme, rosemary and garlic; arrange fish snugly in dish, turning to coat well. Cover and marinate in refrigerator for at least 30 minutes or up to 2 hours.

- Reserving marinade, place fish on greased grill over medium-high heat; sprinkle with salt and pepper to taste. Cook, basting often with marinade, pressing gently to make herbs adhere and turning once with 2 spatulas, for about 8 minutes or until fish flakes easily when tested with fork.

Makes 4 servings.
PER SERVING: about 250 calories, 24 g protein, 16 g fat, 1 g carbohydrate.

TIP: Some firm-fleshed fish suitable for barbecuing are halibut, swordfish, grouper, salmon, tuna, monkfish and Boston bluefish.

Turkey Chili Cornbread Casserole

When the call comes for a potluck supper, win raves with this kernel-studded cornbread topping over nice and spicy turkey chili. Serve with a green salad fancied up with chopped avocado.

1 tbsp	olive oil	15 mL
1	onion, chopped	1
2	cloves garlic, minced	2
Half	jalapeño pepper, seeded and minced	Half
2 tbsp	chili powder	25 mL
¼ tsp	each salt and pepper	1 mL
1	each stalk celery and carrot, chopped	1
1½ lb	lean ground turkey or chicken	750 g
1	can (19 oz/540 mL) Cajun stewed tomatoes	1
1 cup	tomato sauce	250 mL
1	can (19 oz/540 mL) red kidney beans, drained and rinsed	1
¼ cup	chopped fresh coriander	50 mL
CORNBREAD TOPPING:		
2 cups	corn kernels	500 mL
1 cup	all-purpose flour	250 mL
1 cup	buttermilk	250 mL
½ cup	cornmeal	125 mL
1	egg	1
2 tbsp	butter, melted	25 mL
2 tsp	baking powder	10 mL
½ tsp	baking soda	2 mL
½ tsp	salt	2 mL
1½ cups	shredded Monterey Jack or Cheddar cheese	375 mL

- In large deep skillet, heat oil over medium heat; cook onion and garlic, stirring occasionally, for 3 minutes. Add jalapeño, chili powder, salt and pepper; cook, stirring, for 1 minute. Add celery, carrot and turkey; cook, stirring to break up turkey, for about 10 minutes or until no longer pink.

- Stir in tomatoes, breaking up with spoon; stir in tomato sauce. Bring to boil; reduce heat to low and simmer for 5 minutes. Stir in kidney beans and coriander. *(Chili can be cooled in refrigerator, covered and stored for up to 1 day.)* Pour into 13- x 9-inch (3 L) baking dish.

- CORNBREAD TOPPING: In bowl, whisk together corn, flour, buttermilk, cornmeal, egg, butter, baking powder, baking soda and salt; spoon evenly over filling. Sprinkle with cheese.

- Bake in 400°F (200°C) oven for 30 to 35 minutes or until set and deep golden. Let stand for 10 minutes.

Makes 8 servings.

PER SERVING: about 490 calories, 31 g protein, 19 g fat, 49 g carbohydrate, very high source fibre, excellent source calcium and iron.

MAKE-AHEAD SUPPER TIPS

- When cooking pasta for a casserole that is not going to be baked right away, undercook slightly, then rinse under cold water.

- Frozen dishes can take longer to get on the table than you think. Most have to be thawed in the refrigerator for 24 to 48 hours.

- Label frozen food with the name of the dish, the date frozen and the reheating instructions to save time later on.

- When making dishes ahead, always undercook slightly since they will cook more when reheated.

- Don't add bread crumb toppings if freezing a dish; they will become soggy. Add the crumbs just before reheating.

- Add potatoes when reheating a dish since their texture changes when frozen.

- Use only regular or parboiled rice in a dish to be frozen; quick-cooking rice becomes very mushy when frozen.

Basil-Marinated Flank Steak

While flank steak may seem expensive, it is all lean meat, is utterly reliable to cook and here it basks to tender tastiness in a tangy marinade. Great value!

⅓ cup	vegetable oil	75 mL
3 tbsp	red wine vinegar	50 mL
1	clove garlic, minced	1
1 tsp	dried basil	5 mL
1 tsp	Dijon mustard	5 mL
¼ tsp	each pepper and granulated sugar	1 mL
1	flank steak (about 1½ lb/750 g)	1
	Salt	

TIPS
- Always slice flank steak thinly across the grain for maximum tenderness.
- You can freeze the steak in the marinade for up to 2 weeks. Thaw completely in refrigerator, about 24 hours. Let stand at room temperature for 30 minutes.

- In large shallow glass dish, whisk together oil, vinegar, garlic, basil, mustard, pepper and sugar; add steak, turning to coat. Cover and marinate in refrigerator for at least 8 hours or up to 24 hours, turning occasionally. Let stand at room temperature for 30 minutes.

- Reserving marinade, place steak on greased grill over medium-high heat; grill, brushing occasionally with marinade, for 5 to 7 minutes per side for medium-rare or to desired doneness. Transfer to cutting board; tent with foil and let stand for 5 minutes. Season with salt to taste. To serve, slice diagonally across the grain into thin slices.

Makes 6 servings.
PER SERVING: about 275 calories, 26 g protein, 18 g fat,

Plum-Glazed Ribs

A tingly plum-based sauce is an outrageous flatterer when it comes to pork (see photo opposite page).

3 lb	pork spareribs	1.5 kg
¾ cup	plum sauce	175 mL
¼ cup	cider vinegar	50 mL
2 tbsp	tomato paste	25 mL
1 tsp	minced gingerroot	5 mL
1 tsp	Dijon mustard	5 mL
¾ tsp	Worcestershire sauce	4 mL
½ tsp	hot pepper sauce	2 mL
1	clove garlic, minced	1

- Cut spareribs between bones into single ribs. In large pot, cover ribs with salted water and bring to boil; reduce heat, cover and simmer for about 40 minutes or until fork-tender. Drain well and transfer to bowl.

- Whisk together plum sauce, vinegar, tomato paste, ginger, mustard, Worcestershire, hot pepper sauce and garlic; pour over ribs, turning to coat. Cover and marinate in refrigerator for at least 4 hours or up to 24 hours. Let stand at room temperature for 30 minutes.

- Reserving marinade, place ribs on greased grill over medium-high heat; cover barbecue and cook, turning and basting often with marinade, for 10 to 15 minutes or until glazed and browned.

Makes 4 servings.
PER SERVING: about 470 calories, 31 g protein, 30 g fat, 16 g carbohydrate, good source iron.

TIP: When choosing spareribs, remember that those labelled "back" or "baby back" are more expensive but meatier.

Juicy-Good Corn

The key to success when grilling corn is soaking the husks in water. The key to success in keeping the kitchen clean in the summer is removing the corn silk outside — close to the composter.

4	cobs corn (unhusked)	4
3 tbsp	butter	50 mL
1	clove garlic, minced	1
1 tbsp	chopped fresh parsley	15 mL
½ tsp	each salt and pepper	2 mL

- Peel back husks from corn without detaching from cobs; remove silk. Rewrap cobs in husks; soak in water for at least 20 minutes or up to 1 hour. Drain and pat dry.

- Stir together butter, garlic, parsley, salt and pepper. Peel back husks; brush butter mixture evenly over kernels. Fold husks back over cobs; tie tightly with soaked kitchen string.

- Place on greased grill over medium-high heat; cover barbecue and cook, turning often, for about 15 minutes or until browned all over outside and corn is tender.

Makes 4 servings.

PER SERVING: about 210 calories, 4 g protein, 10 g fat, 31 g carbohydrate, high source fibre.

Raspberry and Rosemary Grilled Lamb Chops

This fragrant marinade permeates the lamb, and the grill adds an irresistible smokiness.

2 tbsp	raspberry vinegar	25 mL
1 tbsp	Dijon mustard	15 mL
1 tbsp	soy sauce	15 mL
2 tsp	minced fresh rosemary (or ½ tsp/2 mL dried)	10 mL
1 tsp	olive oil	5 mL
1	clove garlic, minced	1
8	lamb loin chops	8

- In large shallow dish, whisk together vinegar, mustard, soy sauce, rosemary, oil and garlic; add lamb chops in single layer, turning to coat well. Cover and marinate in refrigerator for at least 2 hours or up to 8 hours, turning occasionally.

- Discarding marinade, place chops on greased grill over medium-high heat; cook for about 5 minutes per side for medium-rare or to desired doneness. Transfer to platter; tent with foil and let stand for 5 minutes.

Makes 4 servings.

PER SERVING: about 125 calories, 18 g protein, 5 g fat, trace carbohydrate.

TIP: This lamb makes an ideal make-ahead dish to take to the cottage or camping. Combine the lamb with the marinade in a plastic freezer bag. Seal the bag and freeze for up to 2 weeks, then thaw completely before grilling.

Pacific Rim Chops

A marriage of Asian ingredients accents and tenderizes the lamb.

2 tbsp	rice vinegar or cider vinegar	25 mL
1 tbsp	liquid honey	15 mL
1 tbsp	soy sauce	15 mL
1 tsp	minced gingerroot	5 mL
2	cloves garlic, minced	2
8	lamb loin chops, 1 inch (2.5 cm) thick	8
	Salt and pepper	

TIP: Pork chops are good with this lamb marinade. Choose thick chops, boneless when the budget permits, and grill or broil just until pink inside.

- In large shallow glass dish, whisk together vinegar, honey, soy sauce, ginger and garlic; add lamb chops in single layer, turning to coat well. Cover and marinate at room temperature for 30 minutes or in refrigerator for 4 hours, turning occasionally.

- Reserving marinade, place lamb on broiler rack or greased grill over medium-high heat; cook, brushing occasionally with marinade, for 5 to 7 minutes per side for medium-rare or to desired doneness. Transfer to platter; tent with foil and let stand for 5 minutes. Season with salt and pepper to taste.

Makes 4 servings.
PER SERVING: about 125 calories, 18 g protein, 5 g fat, 1 g carbohydrate.

Lamb Stew with Spring Vegetables

Stews freeze beautifully, especially the meat and sauce. For a fresh touch, add green vegetables when reheating the stew and warm some crusty bread to mop up the fabulous juices.

2½ lb	boneless lamb shoulder	1.25 kg
¼ cup	all-purpose flour	50 mL
3 tbsp	vegetable oil	50 mL
3	onions, sliced	3
2	cloves garlic, minced	2
2½ cups	beef stock	625 mL
2 tbsp	tomato paste	25 mL
1½ tsp	crumbled dried rosemary	7 mL
¾ tsp	salt	4 mL
½ tsp	pepper	2 mL
1 lb	new potatoes (about 4)	500 g
1 lb	asparagus or green beans	500 g
½ lb	baby carrots (about ¾ cup/175 mL)	250 g
1 cup	peas	250 mL

TIP: For a tasty stewing lamb, choose boneless shoulder, which is frequently available frozen. If unavailable, substitute leg. Be sure to trim off any fat from lamb before cutting into cubes.

- Trim lamb; cut into bite-size cubes. In bowl, toss lamb with flour. In Dutch oven, heat half of the oil over medium-high heat; brown meat, in batches and adding more oil if needed. Transfer to plate and set aside.

- Add onions and garlic to pan; cook, stirring occasionally, for 5 minutes or until softened. Add beef stock and tomato paste; bring to boil, stirring to scrape up brown bits.

- Return meat to pan along with rosemary, salt and pepper. Reduce heat to medium-low; cover and simmer for about 1 hour or until meat is tender. *(Stew can be prepared to this point, cooled in refrigerator and frozen for up to 2 weeks. Thaw completely in refrigerator, about 36 hours; reheat over medium-low heat for about 15 minutes, stirring occasionally.)*

- Scrub and cut potatoes into bite-size chunks. Trim asparagus; cut into 1½-inch (4 cm) pieces. In saucepan of boiling salted water, cook potatoes for 6 minutes. Add carrots; cook for 2 minutes. Add asparagus; cook for 4 minutes or until potatoes and carrots are tender. Drain vegetables and add to stew along with peas; heat through.

Makes 6 servings.
PER SERVING: about 450 calories, 34 g protein, 20 g fat, 32 g carbohydrate, high source fibre, excellent source iron.

Peanutty Pork Chops

Take advantage of family packs of pork chops and divide them up to suit your household. The peanut butter marinade keeps the chops moist and juicy.

½ cup	smooth peanut butter	125 mL
¼ cup	water	50 mL
2 tbsp	vegetable oil	25 mL
2 tbsp	rice vinegar, white wine vinegar or cider vinegar	25 mL
2 tbsp	soy sauce	25 mL
1 tbsp	minced gingerroot	15 mL
1 tbsp	hoisin sauce	15 mL
1½ tsp	sesame oil	7 mL
½ tsp	ground coriander	2 mL
1	clove garlic, minced	1
8	pork loin chops (3 lb/1.5 kg)	8

- In shallow glass dish, whisk together peanut butter, water, vegetable oil, vinegar, soy sauce, ginger, hoisin sauce, sesame oil, coriander and garlic; add chops, turning to coat evenly. Cover and marinate in refrigerator for at least 8 hours or up to 24 hours, turning occasionally. Let stand at room temperature for 30 minutes.

- Reserving marinade, place chops on greased grill over medium-high heat; cook, turning once and basting with marinade, for 12 to 15 minutes or until just a hint of pink remains inside. Transfer to platter; tent with foil and let stand for 5 minutes.

Makes 8 servings.
PER SERVING: about 320 calories, 30 g protein, 20 g fat, 5 g carbohydrate.

TIP: Pork chops can be frozen in the marinade for up to 2 weeks. Thaw completely in refrigerator, about 24 hours. Let stand at room temperature for 30 minutes before grilling.

Barbecue Buttermilk Chicken Legs

Another amazing use for buttermilk besides muffins, mashed potatoes and salad dressing is a chicken marinade. Complement it with herbs — basil, rosemary, thyme and oregano are best.

¾ cup	buttermilk	175 mL
2 tbsp	chopped fresh basil (or 2 tsp/10 mL dried)	25 mL
2 tsp	vegetable oil	10 mL
1 tsp	dry mustard	5 mL
2	cloves garlic, minced	2
¼ tsp	each salt and pepper	1 mL
4	chicken legs, skinned	4
FRESH TOMATO SALSA:		
3	plum tomatoes, chopped	3
2 tbsp	chopped fresh basil (or 2 tsp/10 mL dried)	25 mL
1 tsp	lemon juice	5 mL
1 tsp	olive oil	5 mL
¼ tsp	each salt and pepper	1 mL

- In shallow glass dish, whisk together buttermilk, basil, oil, mustard, garlic, salt and pepper; add chicken, turning to coat. Cover and marinate in refrigerator for at least 8 hours or up to 24 hours, turning occasionally. Let stand at room temperature for 30 minutes.

- FRESH TOMATO SALSA: In bowl, stir together tomatoes, basil, lemon juice, oil, salt and pepper. Set aside.

- Reserving marinade, place chicken, meaty side down, on greased grill over medium heat; cover and cook, turning occasionally and brushing with marinade, for 30 to 40 minutes or until juices run clear when chicken is pierced. Serve topped with tomato salsa.

Makes 4 servings.
PER SERVING: about 200 calories, 27 g protein, 8 g fat, 4 g carbohydrate.

Oriental Chicken and Spinach Salad

*The ingredient list looks a tad long, but this fresh,
healthy salad is worth every instant spent measuring.*

3	boneless skinless chicken breasts	3
1	each sweet red and yellow pepper	1
8 cups	torn trimmed spinach	2 L
⅔ cup	snow peas, blanched	150 mL
2	green onions, chopped	2
2 cups	bean sprouts	500 mL
DRESSING:		
⅓ cup	teriyaki sauce	75 mL
¼ cup	fresh coriander leaves	50 mL
2 tbsp	tahini or peanut butter	25 mL
2 tbsp	rice vinegar	25 mL
2 tbsp	dry sherry	25 mL
1 tbsp	each vegetable and sesame oil	15 mL
1 tbsp	liquid honey	15 mL
2	cloves garlic, minced	2
2 tsp	minced gingerroot	10 mL

- DRESSING: In food processor or blender, combine
  teriyaki sauce, coriander, tahini, vinegar, sherry,
  vegetable and sesame oils, honey, garlic and ginger
  until coriander is finely chopped. *(Dressing can be
  covered and refrigerated for up to 8 hours.)*

- In shallow glass dish, pour ¼ cup (50 mL) of the
  dressing over chicken, turning to coat well. Marinate at
  room temperature for 30 minutes.

- Meanwhile, stem and core red and yellow peppers; cut
  into quarters. Cut each quarter in half crosswise; cut
  into thin strips. In large serving bowl, combine
  peppers, spinach, snow peas, onions and bean sprouts.

- Reserving marinade, place chicken on greased grill
  over medium heat; cover and cook, turning once and
  basting with marinade, for 12 minutes or until no
  longer pink inside. Transfer to cutting board; tent with
  foil and let stand for 3 minutes. Slice diagonally into
  strips; add to bowl and toss with remaining dressing.

Makes 4 servings.

PER SERVING: about 315 calories, 29 g protein, 13 g fat,
23 g carbohydrate, very high source fibre, good source
calcium, excellent source iron.

Summery Slaw

Here's a new light version of a make-ahead cabbage salad.

1	each sweet red and green pepper	1
4 cups	finely shredded cabbage	1 L
2	stalks celery, thinly sliced	2
3	green onions, chopped	3
1	carrot, grated	1
DRESSING:		
¼ cup	cider vinegar	50 mL
2 tbsp	apple juice	25 mL
1 tbsp	Dijon mustard	15 mL
½ tsp	celery seeds	2 mL
½ tsp	each salt and pepper	2 mL
3 tbsp	vegetable oil	50 mL

- Stem and core red and green peppers; cut each into quarters. Cut each quarter in half crosswise; cut into thin strips. In bowl, toss together peppers, cabbage, celery, onions and carrot.

- DRESSING: In microwaveable measure or small saucepan, whisk together vinegar, apple juice, mustard, celery seeds, salt and pepper; gradually whisk in oil. Microwave at High for 1 minute or heat over high heat until boiling. Pour over salad; toss well to coat evenly. Cover and refrigerate for at least 2 hours or up to 24 hours.

Makes 4 servings.
PER SERVING: about 150 calories, 2 g protein, 11 g fat, 13 g carbohydrate.

Rice Twice Salad

Brown and white rice unite in a salad that's worth making over and over again. For maximum eye appeal, serve in a bowl lined with Boston or Bibb lettuce.

⅔ cup	each brown and white rice	150 mL
⅓ cup	finely chopped red onion	75 mL
¼ cup	finely chopped carrot	50 mL
DRESSING:		
¼ cup	each chopped fresh parsley and basil (or 2 tsp/10 mL dried)	50 mL
¼ cup	white wine vinegar	50 mL
½ tsp	granulated sugar	2 mL
½ tsp	each salt and pepper	2 mL
1	clove garlic, minced	1
⅓ cup	olive oil	75 mL

- In large saucepan, bring 2⅔ cups (650 mL) salted water to boil. Stir in brown rice; return to boil. Reduce heat, cover and simmer for 15 minutes. Stir in white rice; cook, covered, for about 20 minutes or until brown and white rice are tender and liquid is absorbed. Transfer to large bowl; let cool to room temperature.

- DRESSING: In bowl, whisk together parsley, basil, vinegar, sugar, salt, pepper and garlic; gradually whisk in oil.

- Add onion, carrot and three-quarters of the dressing to rice; toss gently. *(Salad can be covered and refrigerated for up to 2 days.)* Just before serving, toss with remaining dressing.

Makes 6 servings.
PER SERVING: about 270 calories, 4 g protein, 13 g fat, 35 g carbohydrate.

TIP: This recipe is a great way to use up leftover rice; use 2½ cups (625 mL) each cooked brown and white rice.

Minted Couscous Salad

Salads can be every bit as memorable as the main course, as this summery dish, with its palette of colors and generous nod to fresh herbs, can attest.

1⅓ cups	chicken stock or water	325 mL
1 cup	couscous	250 mL
½ cup	raisins (optional)	125 mL
2	green onions, chopped	2
2	stalks celery, finely chopped	2
1	large carrot, finely chopped	1
1	sweet red or yellow pepper, diced	1
DRESSING:		
2 tbsp	white wine vinegar	25 mL
1 tsp	Dijon mustard	5 mL
1 tsp	lemon juice	5 mL
¾ tsp	ginger	4 mL
¼ tsp	salt	1 mL
Pinch	pepper	Pinch
⅓ cup	olive oil	75 mL
¼ cup	chopped fresh mint	50 mL
	Sprigs fresh mint	

- In saucepan, bring chicken stock to boil; stir in couscous, and raisins (if using). Remove from heat; cover and let stand for 5 minutes. Fluff with fork; transfer to bowl. Stir in onions, celery, carrot and red pepper. *(Salad can be prepared to this point, covered and refrigerated for up to 8 hours.)*

- DRESSING: In small bowl, whisk together vinegar, mustard, lemon juice, ginger, salt and pepper; gradually whisk in oil. Whisk in three-quarters of the chopped mint. *(Dressing can be covered and refrigerated for up to 8 hours; whisk before using.)*

- Toss couscous mixture with dressing. Sprinkle with remaining chopped mint; garnish with mint sprigs.

  Makes 4 servings.
  PER SERVING: about 375 calories, 8 g protein, 19 g fat, 43 g carbohydrate, high source fibre.

Dilled Potato and Apple Salad

Apple may seem unusual in a potato salad, but with the dill and radishes, it adds a fresh taste.

3	large new potatoes	3
6	radishes	6
1	each carrot and stalk celery	1
Half	apple (unpeeled)	Half
¼ cup	finely chopped Spanish onion	50 mL
¼ cup	chopped fresh dill	50 mL
⅓ cup	light sour cream	75 mL
⅓ cup	low-fat plain yogurt	75 mL
2 tsp	Dijon mustard	10 mL
½ tsp	salt	2 mL
¼ tsp	pepper	1 mL

- In pot of boiling salted water, cook potatoes, covered, for about 20 minutes or until tender. Drain and return to pot over medium heat for 1 minute to dry. Let cool slightly; peel and cut into bite-size chunks.

- Meanwhile, coarsely chop radishes, carrot, celery and apple. Place in bowl along with potatoes, onion and dill.

- Whisk together sour cream, yogurt, mustard, salt and pepper; pour over potato mixture and toss gently to combine. Cover and refrigerate for at least 1 hour or up to 24 hours.

  Makes 4 servings.
  PER SERVING: about 190 calories, 6 g protein, 2 g fat, 39 g carbohydrate, high source fibre.

Carol Ferguson's Country Kitchen Pea Soup

Early on, Canadian Living's founding food editor, Carol Ferguson, vowed to create the best possible rendition of traditional dishes and that's what she did with this Quebec specialty.

1 lb	dried whole yellow peas	500 g
½ lb	piece salt pork	250 g
1	large onion, chopped	1
½ cup	chopped celery (with leaves)	125 mL
¼ cup	chopped fresh parsley	50 mL
1	bay leaf	1
2 tsp	salt	10 mL
1 tsp	dried savory	5 mL
	Salt and pepper	

- Wash and sort peas, discarding any blemished ones. Cover with cold water and let soak overnight.

- Measure water in which peas have soaked; add enough fresh water to make 12 cups (3 L) and pour into large pot. Add peas, salt pork, onion, celery, parsley, bay leaf, salt and savory; bring to boil. Reduce heat to low; cover and simmer for about 2 hours or until peas are tender.

- Remove about 2 cups (500 mL) of the peas; mash or purée in blender and return to soup. Season with salt and pepper to taste. Discard bay leaf. Remove pork; chop and return to soup, or slice and serve separately.

Makes 8 servings.
PER SERVING: about 415 calories, 15 g protein, 24 g fat, 37 g carbohydrate, very high source fibre, good source iron.

TIP: This soup is very good reheated.

Chunky Chicken Soup with Winter Vegetables

This hearty soup is chock-full of tender chunks of chicken and colorful vegetables.

1	chicken (about 3 lb/1.5 kg)	1
	Salt and pepper	
2	onions, halved	2
6	cloves garlic	6
2	bay leaves	2
8 cups	chicken stock	2 L
1 tsp	dried thyme	5 mL
½ tsp	dried sage	2 mL
4	carrots, cut in bite-size chunks	4
4	stalks celery (with leaves), cut in bite-size chunks	4
2	leeks, quartered and cut in 1-inch (2.5 cm) lengths	2
2	parsnips, peeled and cut in bite-size chunks	2
Half	rutabaga, peeled and cut in bite-size pieces	Half
2 tbsp	chopped fresh parsley	25 mL

- Remove fat from chicken; sprinkle inside and out with salt and pepper. Place in large saucepan. Add onions, garlic and bay leaves. Pour in stock; bring to boil, skimming foam from top. Add thyme and sage; cover and cook over low heat for 30 minutes.

- Add carrots, celery, leeks, parsnips and rutabaga; simmer, covered, for 35 to 45 minutes or until vegetables are tender and chicken is coming off bones. Discard bay leaves and onions; skim off fat. Remove chicken and let stand until cool enough to handle; remove meat from bones and tear into large pieces, discarding skin. Add pieces to stock. *(Soup can be cooled in refrigerator, covered and stored in airtight container for up to 2 days. Discard any remaining fat on broth; reheat gently over low heat).* Sprinkle with parsley.

Makes 8 servings.
PER SERVING: about 250 calories, 25 g protein, 8 g fat, 19 g carbohydrate, high source fibre, good source iron.

Penne Siciliana

An excellent frozen dinner to keep on hand, this robust Sicilian pasta travels well, too.

1 tbsp	olive oil	15 mL
2	cloves garlic, minced	2
1	can (28 oz/796 mL) tomatoes (undrained), coarsely chopped	1
⅓ cup	sun-dried tomatoes, slivered	75 mL
½ tsp	each dried oregano and thyme	2 mL
⅓ cup	finely chopped fresh parsley	75 mL
1	jar (6 oz/170 mL) marinated artichoke hearts, drained and quartered	1
2 tbsp	small capers, rinsed	25 mL
½ cup	Kalamata olives, pitted and quartered	125 mL
5 cups	penne pasta	1.25 L
	Salt and pepper	

- In large skillet, heat oil over medium heat; cook garlic, stirring, for 1 minute. Add tomatoes, sun-dried tomatoes, oregano and thyme; bring to boil. Reduce heat to medium; simmer for 10 minutes or until thickened.

- Add parsley, artichoke hearts and capers; cook, stirring occasionally, for 10 minutes. *(Sauce can be prepared to this point, cooled in refrigerator and frozen in airtight container for up to 2 weeks; thaw and reheat over low heat.)* Stir in olives.

- Meanwhile, in large pot of boiling salted water, cook penne for 8 to 10 minutes or until tender but firm; drain well and toss with sauce. Season with salt and pepper to taste.

Makes 4 servings.

PER SERVING: about 645 calories, 20 g protein, 15 g fat, 110 g carbohydrate, very high source fibre, excellent source iron.

TIP: To pit olives, press olive firmly with flat knife blade on cutting board; remove pit with fingers. Also, use scissors to cut sun-dried tomatoes easily.

Double Tomato Sauce over Polenta

Tomato sauce enriched by sun-dried tomatoes waits without worry for a day or two in the refrigerator, longer in the freezer. It's a natural over pasta, but what about polenta?

1 tbsp	olive oil	15 mL
1	onion, chopped	1
2	cloves garlic, minced	2
Pinch	each paprika and cayenne	Pinch
1	can (28 oz/796 mL) tomatoes	1
8	sun-dried tomatoes, sliced	8
	Freshly grated Parmesan cheese (optional)	
POLENTA:		
1 tbsp	olive oil	15 mL
1	onion, chopped	1
6 cups	chicken or vegetable stock	1.5 L
1½ cups	cornmeal	375 mL
¼ cup	freshly grated Parmesan cheese	50 mL
1 tbsp	butter	15 mL

- In heavy saucepan, heat oil over medium heat; cook onion, garlic, paprika and cayenne, stirring often, for 5 minutes.

- Add tomatoes, crushing coarsely with fork; add sun-dried tomatoes. Bring to boil; reduce heat and simmer for 30 minutes or until thickened.

- POLENTA: Meanwhile, in heavy saucepan, heat oil over medium heat; cook onion, stirring occasionally, for 4 minutes. Pour in stock; bring to boil. Gradually whisk in cornmeal; cook, stirring constantly, for about 15 minutes or until smooth and thick enough to mound stiffly on spoon. Mix in Parmesan cheese and butter.

- Spoon polenta into 4 bowls; top with sauce. Sprinkle with Parmesan cheese if desired.

Makes 4 servings.

PER SERVING: about 435 calories, 18 g protein, 15 g fat, 58 g carbohydrate, very high source fibre, good source calcium and iron.

Italian Pasta and Spinach Casserole

Every household's make-ahead repertoire should include this simple, all-age-pleasing casserole. Why not make two, one for now, and one for later?

1 tbsp	vegetable oil	15 mL
1½ lb	lean ground beef	750 g
1	onion, chopped	1
2	cloves garlic, minced	2
3 cups	sliced mushrooms (½ lb/250 g)	750 mL
1	can (28 oz/796 mL) tomatoes	1
¼ cup	tomato paste	50 mL
1 tsp	each dried basil and oregano	5 mL
¾ tsp	salt	4 mL
½ tsp	pepper	2 mL
1 tbsp	red wine vinegar	15 mL
4 cups	small shell pasta	1 L
½ cup	bread crumbs	125 mL
¼ cup	freshly grated Parmesan cheese	50 mL

FILLING:

1	pkg (10 oz/300 g) fresh spinach	1
1 cup	cottage cheese	250 mL
2 tbsp	milk	25 mL
¼ cup	freshly grated Parmesan cheese	50 mL
¼ tsp	pepper	1 mL

- FILLING: Rinse spinach; shake off excess water. In large covered saucepan, cook spinach over medium-high heat, with just the water clinging to leaves, for about 4 minutes or until wilted. Drain well and squeeze dry; coarsely chop and place in bowl.

- In blender or food processor, purée cottage cheese with milk until smooth. Add to spinach along with Parmesan cheese and pepper. Set aside.

- In large saucepan, heat oil over medium-high heat; cook beef, onion, garlic and mushrooms, stirring occasionally and breaking up meat, for 7 to 10 minutes or until beef is no longer pink. Skim off any fat. Add tomatoes, breaking up with fork. Add tomato paste, basil, oregano, salt and pepper; bring to boil. Reduce heat and simmer for 20 minutes or until thickened. Stir in vinegar.

- Meanwhile, in large pot of boiling salted water, cook pasta for about 8 minutes or until tender but firm. Drain well; stir into meat sauce.

- Spread one-quarter of the pasta mixture in each of 2 greased 8-inch (2 L) square baking dishes. Divide spinach mixture between dishes, spreading evenly. Top with remaining pasta mixture. *(Casseroles can be prepared to this point, covered and frozen for up to 2 weeks. Thaw completely in refrigerator, about 36 hours.)*

- Sprinkle with bread crumbs and Parmesan cheese. Bake, covered, in 350°F (180°C) oven for 30 minutes (or 55 to 60 minutes if casserole had been frozen) or until heated through, uncovering for last 15 minutes.

Makes 8 servings.

PER SERVING: about 470 calories, 31 g protein, 18 g fat, 44 g carbohydrate, high source fibre, good source calcium, excellent source iron.

Primavera Lasagna

Meaning "spring-style," primavera uses fresh or blanched vegetables. A busy mother, home economist
Heather Howe perfected this dish for entertaining.

2	carrots, chopped	2
1 lb	asparagus, cut in 1 ½-inch (4 cm) pieces	500 g
2	zucchini, chopped	2
1 cup	peas	250 mL
⅓ cup	butter	75 mL
3	large cloves garlic, minced	3
1	onion, chopped	1
1 tbsp	dried marjoram	15 mL
½ cup	all-purpose flour	125 mL
3 cups	milk	750 mL
1	pkg (8 oz/250 g) cream cheese, cubed	1
3 tbsp	lemon juice	50 mL
1½ tsp	salt	7 mL
¾ tsp	pepper	4 mL
15	lasagna noodles	15
2 cups	shredded Gruyère cheese	500 mL
½ cup	freshly grated Parmesan cheese	125 mL

- In large saucepan of boiling water, cook carrots for 3 minutes. Add asparagus, zucchini and peas; cook for 1 minute. Drain, reserving 2 cups (500 mL) liquid. Refresh under cold water; drain again.

- In saucepan, melt butter over medium heat; cook garlic, onion and marjoram, stirring occasionally, for about 3 minutes or until onion is softened.

- Gradually whisk in flour; cook, stirring, for 1 minute. Whisk in milk and reserved cooking liquid; bring to boil, whisking. Reduce heat to medium-low; cook, stirring, for 10 minutes or until thickened. Whisk in cream cheese until melted. Remove from heat; stir in lemon juice, salt and pepper.

- Meanwhile, in large pot of boiling salted water, cook noodles for about 10 minutes or until tender but firm. Drain and rinse under cold water; drain and pat dry.

- Arrange 3 noodles in greased 13- x 9-inch (3 L) baking dish. Spread with 1 cup (250 mL) of the sauce, then one-quarter of the vegetables, then one-quarter of the Gruyère cheese. Repeat layers 3 more times. Top with final layer of noodles and remaining sauce. Sprinkle with Parmesan cheese. *(Lasagna can be prepared to this point, covered and frozen for up to 2 weeks. Thaw completely in refrigerator, about 48 hours.)*

- Bake, uncovered, on baking sheet in 375°F (190°C) oven for 35 to 40 minutes (or 60 to 70 minutes if lasagna had been frozen) or until bubbly and golden. Let stand for 20 minutes before serving.

Makes 8 servings.
PER SERVING: about 620 calories, 26 g protein, 33 g fat, 56 g carbohydrate, high source fibre, excellent source calcium, good source iron.

FREEZING TIPS FOR CASSEROLES AND STEWS

- Line baking dishes with foil before filling. Once frozen, lift block out using foil as handles and rewrap tightly for storage. The frozen block can be returned to the same dish for thawing and reheating. Foil pans also make great containers.

- Wrap securely in plastic wrap then foil to prevent any air from getting in.

- Label and date before freezing for easy identification.

- Thaw in refrigerator rather than on the counter; this can take up to 48 hours depending on the density of the food.

Italian Meatball Shepherd's Pie

Creamy mashed potatoes enriched with Parmesan cheese top a layer of Italian-style meatballs.
This is the ultimate in comfy casseroles.

1 lb	lean ground beef	500 g
2	cloves garlic, minced	2
	Salt and pepper	
2 tbsp	all-purpose flour	25 mL
1 tbsp	olive oil	15 mL
1	small onion, chopped	1
1½ cups	canned tomatoes	375 mL
½ tsp	each dried basil and oregano	2 mL
3	large baking potatoes, peeled and quartered	3
1	egg, beaten	1
1 cup	freshly grated Parmesan cheese	250 mL
2 tbsp	chopped fresh parsley	25 mL

- In bowl, mix together beef, half of the garlic, ¼ tsp (1 mL) each salt and pepper and 2 tbsp (25 mL) cold water; gently form into 1 ½-inch (4 cm) balls.

- In shallow dish, combine flour with pinch each salt and pepper; roll meatballs in flour to coat.

- In large nonstick skillet, heat half of the oil over medium heat; cook meatballs, in batches, until browned all over. Remove to plate and set aside.

- Add remaining oil to skillet; cook onion and remaining garlic, stirring occasionally, for 5 minutes. Stir in tomatoes, basil, oregano and meatballs; simmer, uncovered and stirring often, for 15 minutes.

- Meanwhile, in saucepan of boiling water, cook potatoes for 20 minutes or until tender. Drain well; mash until smooth. Stir in egg, ¾ cup (175 mL) of the Parmesan cheese, and salt and pepper to taste. Stir in parsley.

- Spoon meatball mixture into 8-inch (2 L) square baking dish. Spread potato mixture over top. Sprinkle with remaining Parmesan. *(Casserole can be prepared to this point, covered and refrigerated for up to 1 day; bring to room temperature.)*

- Cover and bake in 350°F (180°C) oven for 45 minutes. Uncover and bake for 10 minutes. Broil for 1 minute or until cheese is golden.

Makes 4 servings.
PER SERVING: about 515 calories, 37 g protein, 25 g fat, 35 g carbohydrate, excellent source calcium and iron.

CHAPTER FIVE

GETTING TOGETHER IS FUN

*When the accent is on
easy-to-prepare dishes,
helping hands in the kitchen
and delicious tastes with
universal appeal, entertaining
is more than just fun, it's a joy.*

Cajun Fish Kabobs

A mix of spicy and hot, but not too hot, makes Cajun one cool flavor. Fish prepared this quick way is low in fat and can be broiled when it's too cold to barbecue.

1 tbsp	olive oil	15 mL
1	clove garlic, minced	1
1 tsp	paprika	5 mL
¾ tsp	pepper	4 mL
½ tsp	each dry mustard and dried oregano	2 mL
½ tsp	chili powder	2 mL
¼ tsp	salt	1 mL
Pinch	cayenne pepper	Pinch
1 lb	salmon fillet, skinned	500 g

- In bowl, stir together oil, garlic, paprika, pepper, mustard, oregano, chili powder, salt and cayenne.
- Cut salmon into 1½-inch (4 cm) chunks; add to bowl and gently toss to coat evenly. Thread onto 4 soaked wooden skewers.
- Place kabobs on greased grill over medium heat; cover and cook, turning once, for about 6 minutes or until opaque and fish flakes easily when tested with fork.

Makes 4 servings.
PER SERVING: about 185 calories, 21 g protein, 10 g fat, 1 g carbohydrate.

TIP: **To prevent wooden skewers from charring while on the barbecue, soak them in water for at least 30 minutes before using.**

Steamed Fish with Tangy Vinaigrette

A simple vinaigrette replaces a rich sauce for steamed fish.

1 lb	thick fish fillets	500 g
3 tbsp	red wine vinegar	50 mL
3 tbsp	rice vinegar	50 mL
2 tbsp	finely chopped red onion	25 mL
1 tbsp	chopped fresh dill	15 mL
1 tsp	capers	5 mL
1 tsp	each chopped fresh basil and chives	5 mL
¼ tsp	each salt and pepper	1 mL
¼ cup	olive oil	50 mL

- In steamer, steam fish for 5 to 10 minutes or until fish flakes easily when tested with fork.
- Meanwhile, in blender, purée together red wine vinegar, rice vinegar, onion, dill, capers, basil, chives, salt and pepper; with machine running, gradually pour in oil. Drizzle over fish.

Makes 4 servings.
PER SERVING: about 250 calories, 24 g protein, 16 g fat, 2 g carbohydrate.

Salmon and Wild Rice Pie

Potluck fare par excellence! This sturdy and hearty all-season pie is for big appetites.
Balance your menu with a light salad and dessert of fruit.

¾ cup	wild rice	175 mL
2 tbsp	butter	25 mL
4	green onions, sliced	4
2½ cups	sliced mushrooms	625 mL
2	stalks celery, diced	2
2 tbsp	chopped fresh dill (or 2 tsp/10 mL dried dillweed)	25 mL
2 tbsp	chopped fresh parsley	25 mL
1 tsp	salt	5 mL
¼ tsp	pepper	1 mL
4	cans (each 213 g) sockeye salmon	4
4	eggs	4
1¼ cups	light sour cream	300 mL
	Pastry for deep 10-inch (25 cm) double-crust pie (see Perfect Pastry, page 168)	
1 tsp	milk	5 mL

- Rinse rice. In small saucepan, cover rice with 4 cups (1 L) water; bring to boil. Reduce heat, cover and simmer for 45 minutes or just until tender; drain and transfer to large bowl.

- Meanwhile, in large skillet, melt butter over medium heat; cook onions, mushrooms and celery, stirring often, for about 10 minutes or until softened and liquid is evaporated. Let cool. Add to rice along with dill, parsley, salt and pepper.

- Drain salmon, discarding any skin and mashing bones; gently stir into rice. *(Filling can be prepared to this point, covered and refrigerated for up to 8 hours.)* In small bowl, beat 3 of the eggs; blend in sour cream. Gently stir into rice mixture.

- On lightly floured surface, roll out half of the pastry and line deep 10-inch (25 cm) pie plate; spoon in filling and pat down. Roll out remaining pastry. Moisten pastry rim; arrange pastry over filling. Trim and flute edge.

- Beat remaining egg with milk; brush over pastry. Cut steam vents in top. Bake in 400°F (200°C) oven for 15 minutes. Reduce heat to 375°F (190°C); bake for about 35 minutes longer or until golden. Let stand for 30 minutes before serving.

Makes 8 servings.
PER SERVING: about 575 calories, 29 g protein, 33 g fat, 39 g carbohydrate, excellent source calcium, good source iron.

TIP: If making pastry is not your forte, cheat and use two store-bought frozen deep-dish pie shells. Thaw them for 20 minutes before filling one and inverting the other over top of the filling.

BUYING AND COOKING WILD RICE

- Wild rice, which is not a rice at all but rather the grainlike seed of an aquatic grass, *Zizania aquatica,* is indigenous to the northern Great Lakes area, where it's grown commercially, as well as to the Lac la Ronge area of Saskatchewan. It is shiny black and needlelike and has a nutty flavor. Rinse thoroughly before cooking.

- Wild rice is available at most supermarkets. Although expensive, a little goes a long way; it expands four times when cooked. You can also mix it with long-grain rice to make it go further.

- It takes a little longer to cook than long-grain rice does; it's cooked when it starts to split.

Scallops for Two

Scallops are a bit of a splurge, so why not enjoy this low-fat, fresh-tasting salad for a special occasion.

½ lb	asparagus, trimmed	250 g
½ lb	bay scallops	250 g
Half	small red onion	Half
1	orange	1
1	small head Boston lettuce	1
DRESSING:		
2 tbsp	orange juice	25 mL
1 ½ tsp	grated lime or lemon rind	7 mL
1 tbsp	lime or lemon juice	15 mL
1 tbsp	rice vinegar or cider vinegar	15 mL
1 tbsp	vegetable oil	15 mL
1 tsp	liquid honey	5 mL
¼ tsp	salt	1 mL
1 tbsp	each chopped fresh parsley and mint	15 mL

- In steamer, steam asparagus for 4 minutes or just until tender-crisp. Refresh under cold water; drain well and place in large bowl.

- In saucepan, cover scallops with cold water; bring to boil. Reduce heat and simmer for about 1 minute or just until opaque in centre. Drain and refresh under cold water; drain again and add to bowl.

- Slice half of the onion into rings; add to bowl. Chop remaining onion finely; set aside. Peel orange and remove outside membrane. Slice into rounds; cut in half and add to bowl.

- DRESSING: In small bowl, combine orange juice, lime rind and juice, vinegar, oil, honey and salt; stir in parsley, mint and chopped onion. Pour over asparagus mixture.

- Separate lettuce into leaves; arrange on plates. With slotted spoon, arrange asparagus mixture on top; drizzle with dressing.

Makes 2 servings.
PER SERVING: about 270 calories, 24 g protein, 8 g fat, 28 g carbohydrate, high source fibre.

Barbecued Salmon

Shirl Hall of the Heiltsuk Cultural Centre in British Columbia is the source of this very simple and delicious traditional recipe.

1 ½ lb	salmon fillet (skin on)	750 g
½ tsp	salt	2 mL

- Cut slit through skin at each end of salmon fillet; thread fillet lengthwise onto metal skewer. Sprinkle with salt.

- Place fillet, skin side down, on greased grill; cover and cook for 12 to 20 minutes or until fish is opaque and flakes easily when tested with fork.

Makes 8 servings.
PER SERVING: about 110 calories, 15 g protein, 5 g fat, no carbohydrate.

TIP: Adding wood chips, such as mesquite or hickory, to the barbecue's hot lava rocks or coals adds a wonderful smoky dimension to food. Soak the chips in hot water for 30 minutes, then add directly to the coals; heat until the chips begin to smoke before adding the food to the grill.

Linguine with Shrimp and Basil

Pasta is a healthy choice for company meals. Tomato is a low-fat topping, and this dish,
with a company touch of shrimp, delivers protein, iron and fibre, too.

1	can (28 oz/796 mL) tomatoes	1
1	can (5½ oz/156 mL) tomato paste	1
½ cup	chopped fresh basil (or 1 tbsp/15 mL dried)	125 mL
4	cloves garlic, minced	4
1	onion, chopped	1
1 tbsp	chopped fresh oregano (or 1 tsp/5 mL dried)	15 mL
1 lb	large raw shrimp, peeled and deveined	500 g
¾ lb	linguine	375 g

- In saucepan, mash tomatoes with juice; stir in tomato paste, half of the basil, the garlic, onion and oregano. Bring to boil; reduce heat and simmer, stirring occasionally, for 20 minutes or until onion is tender and sauce has thickened slightly.

- Add shrimp; cover and cook for about 3 minutes or just until shrimp are pink.

- Meanwhile, in large pot of boiling salted water, cook linguine for 8 to 10 minutes or until tender but firm; drain well and toss with sauce and remaining basil.

Makes 4 servings.

PER SERVING: about 530 calories, 38 g protein, 4 g fat, 85 g carbohydrate, very high source fibre, excellent source iron.

Szechuan Barbecued Chicken

Chicken breasts with the bone in always have more flavor and they stay moister too, especially on the barbecue.

4	chicken breasts	4
3 tbsp	sherry or chicken stock	50 mL
3 tbsp	soy sauce	50 mL
2 tbsp	hoisin sauce	25 mL
1 tbsp	balsamic or red wine vinegar	15 mL
1 tbsp	sesame oil	15 mL
3	green onions, minced	3
1	large clove garlic, minced	1
1 tbsp	minced gingerroot	15 mL
Pinch	hot pepper flakes	Pinch

TIP: When barbecuing, be sure to use a clean platter to serve cooked chicken, never the same plate that was used to hold the raw chicken.

- Arrange chicken in single layer in shallow glass dish. Whisk together sherry, soy sauce, hoisin sauce, vinegar, oil, green onions, garlic, ginger and hot pepper flakes; pour over chicken, turning to coat well.

- Cover and marinate in refrigerator for at least 8 hours or up to 24 hours. Let stand at room temperature for 30 minutes.

- Reserving marinade, place chicken on greased grill over medium heat; cover and cook, basting with marinade and turning occasionally, for 25 to 30 minutes or until chicken is no longer pink inside.

Makes 4 servings.
PER SERVING: about 245 calories, 30 g protein, 10 g fat, 4 g carbohydrate.

Stir-Fry Noodles with Chicken

Stir-frying is last-minute, but you can get a jump start by preparing both the sauce and noodles ahead.

¾ lb	spaghettini or Chinese egg noodles	375 g
1 tbsp	(approx) vegetable oil	15 mL
1 lb	boneless skinless chicken breasts, cut in thin strips	500 g
2	cloves garlic, minced	2
1 tbsp	chopped gingerroot	15 mL
¼ tsp	hot pepper flakes	1 mL
6	green onions, chopped	6
2	onions, slivered	2
2	sweet green peppers, cut in strips	2
1	sweet red pepper, cut in strips	1
¼ cup	chopped fresh coriander or parsley	50 mL
PEANUT SAUCE:		
½ cup	warm water	125 mL
½ cup	peanut butter	125 mL
2 tbsp	soy sauce	25 mL
2 tbsp	rice vinegar	25 mL
1 tbsp	frozen orange juice concentrate, thawed	15 mL
1 tbsp	sesame oil	15 mL

- In pot of boiling salted water, cook spaghettini for 8 to 10 minutes or until tender but firm; drain and rinse under cold water. Drain again. *(Pasta can be tossed with 1 tbsp/15 mL vegetable oil, covered and refrigerated for up to 12 hours.)*

- Peanut Sauce: Meanwhile, in bowl, whisk together water, peanut butter, soy sauce, vinegar, orange juice concentrate and sesame oil. *(Sauce can be covered and refrigerated for up to 12 hours.)*

- Meanwhile, brush wok or large nonstick skillet with 1 tbsp (15 mL) oil; heat over medium-high heat until smoking. Stir-fry chicken until lightly browned. Add garlic, ginger, hot pepper flakes and green onions; stir-fry for 3 minutes or until fragrant. Add slivered onions, and green and red peppers; stir-fry for 5 minutes.

- Add peanut sauce and bring to boil; reduce heat and simmer for 5 minutes, adding a little water if sauce thickens too much. Add spaghettini; cook, tossing to coat, for about 5 minutes or until steaming hot. Sprinkle with coriander.

Makes 6 servings.
PER SERVING: about 505 calories, 32 g protein, 17 g fat, 57 g carbohydrate, high source fibre, good source iron.

Lemon Thyme Chicken with Mushrooms

The best thing about chicken is its many different tastes. For entertaining, a lemon-wine marinade turns into a quick sauce for boneless breasts that taste exceptionally good (see photo opposite title page).

6	boneless skinless chicken breasts	6
¼ cup	white wine	50 mL
3 tbsp	olive oil	50 mL
2 tsp	grated lemon rind	10 mL
2 tbsp	lemon juice	25 mL
1 tbsp	chopped fresh thyme (or 1 tsp/5 mL dried)	15 mL
1 tsp	cracked black peppercorns	5 mL
2	cloves garlic, minced	2
½ tsp	Dijon mustard	2 mL
Pinch	granulated sugar	Pinch
3 cups	sliced mushrooms	750 mL
½ cup	chicken stock	125 mL
1 tbsp	butter, in pieces	15 mL
2 tbsp	capers	25 mL
	Salt	

- Arrange chicken in single layer in glass baking dish. Whisk together wine, 2 tbsp (25 mL) of the oil, lemon rind and juice, thyme, peppercorns, garlic, mustard and sugar; pour over chicken. Cover and marinate at room temperature for 20 minutes, turning once.

- In large skillet, heat remaining oil over medium-high heat; cook mushrooms, stirring occasionally, for about 3 minutes or until golden. Transfer to plate; cover and keep warm.

- Reserving marinade, add chicken to pan; cook for about 5 minutes on each side or until golden and no longer pink inside. Add to plate; cover and keep warm.

- Add stock and reserved marinade to pan; bring to boil, stirring to scrape up brown bits. Cook for 3 minutes. Whisk in butter just until melted. Add capers. Return chicken and mushrooms to pan along with any juices; cook, turning chicken to coat, for about 1 minute or until hot. Season with salt to taste.

Makes 6 servings.
PER SERVING: about 230 calories, 28 g protein, 10 g fat, 3 g carbohydrate.

Wilted Greens with Garlic

We have recently discovered just how nutrient-rich greens such as Swiss chard, beet tops, rapini and spinach are. Cook them quickly to retain their precious vitamin C.

1½ lb	greens (Swiss chard, beet greens, rapini or spinach)	750 g
2 tbsp	olive oil	25 mL
2	cloves garlic, minced	2
	Salt and pepper	

TIP: Two bunches of Swiss chard weigh about 1½ lb (750 g), as do the tops from 8 medium-large beets. If measuring by volume, you need what seems like an enormous amount, about 28 cups (7 L).

- Trim stems from greens; cut stems into 1-inch (2.5 cm) pieces.

- In large saucepan, heat oil over medium-high heat; cook garlic, stirring, for 30 seconds. Add stems, and salt and pepper to taste; cook for 2 minutes.

- Arrange leaf greens over top and reduce heat to medium; cover and cook for 5 to 7 minutes or until wilted.

Makes 6 servings.
PER SERVING: about 65 calories, 2 g protein, 5 g fat, 5 g carbohydrate.

Balsamic Chicken and Roasted Vegetables

Balsamic vinegar, like pesto, is an enduring contribution of Italian cooking. Let this dark, almost thick vinegar glamorize three thoroughly regular ingredients — chicken, tomatoes and mushrooms.

4	plum tomatoes	4
12	mushrooms	12
3 tbsp	freshly grated Parmesan cheese	50 mL
4	chicken breasts	4
	Salt and pepper	
SAUCE:		
⅓ cup	balsamic vinegar	75 mL
⅓ cup	tomato juice	75 mL
3 tbsp	olive oil	50 mL
2 tbsp	chopped fresh thyme (or 2 tsp/10 mL dried)	25 mL
2 tbsp	Dijon mustard	25 mL
1 tbsp	granulated sugar	15 mL
2	cloves garlic, minced	2

- SAUCE: In small saucepan, whisk together vinegar, tomato juice, oil, thyme, mustard, sugar and garlic; bring to boil over high heat. Boil, whisking occasionally, for 5 minutes or until thick enough to coat back of spoon. Set ¼ cup (50 mL) aside to serve with chicken.

- Halve tomatoes lengthwise. Remove mushroom stems. Arrange vegetables, cut side up, in 13- x 9-inch (3.5 L) cake pan. Spoon half of the sauce over mushrooms only; sprinkle both vegetables with cheese. Bake on lower rack in 400°F (200°C) oven for 10 minutes.

- Pull off skin from chicken; score meat 3 times. Coat with some of the remaining sauce. Broil, turning and brushing with sauce once, for 12 to 15 minutes or until no longer pink inside. Season chicken and vegetables with salt and pepper to taste. Serve with reserved sauce.

Makes 4 servings.
PER SERVING: about 290 calories, 31 g protein, 14 g fat, 11 g carbohydrate, good source iron.

Lemon Pepper Chicken

You never have to worry about leftovers with this chicken recipe. However, if you are lucky enough to have any, make great sandwiches or salads the next day.

4	chicken legs	4
1 tbsp	grated lemon rind	15 mL
¼ cup	lemon juice	50 mL
2 tbsp	olive oil	25 mL
2 tsp	cracked black peppercorns	10 mL
Half	small onion, minced	Half
1	clove garlic, minced	1
	Salt and pepper	

TIP: To bake, place on foil-lined baking sheet and bake in 375°F (190°C) oven for 35 minutes, basting with marinade.

• Pull off skin from chicken; place in shallow dish. Whisk together lemon rind and juice, oil, pepper, onion and garlic; pour over chicken, turning to coat well. Cover and marinate in refrigerator for 2 hours. Let stand at room temperature for 30 minutes.

• Brush marinade from chicken and reserve. Place chicken, meaty side up, on greased grill over medium heat; cover and cook, turning and basting occasionally with marinade, for about 25 minutes or until juices run clear when chicken is pierced. Season with salt and pepper to taste.

Makes 4 servings.
PER SERVING: about 180 calories, 26 g protein, 7 g fat, 1 g carbohydrate.

Chicken with Mushrooms

The taste of chicken legs and thighs belies their budget price tag. Here's a perfect dish in which to try some of the new mushrooms, such as portobello, shiitake and oyster, for their woodsier flavor.

4	chicken legs	4
¼ cup	all-purpose flour	50 mL
¾ tsp	dried thyme	4 mL
¼ tsp	pepper	1 mL
1 tbsp	vegetable oil	15 mL
1	onion, chopped	1
6 cups	thickly sliced mushrooms (1 lb/500 g)	1.5 L
½ cup	apple juice	125 mL
1 tbsp	balsamic or cider vinegar	15 mL
¼ tsp	salt	1 mL
	Chopped fresh parsley	

• Pull off skin from chicken; separate legs at joint. In plastic bag, combine flour, thyme and pepper; add chicken, in batches if necessary, shaking to coat well.

• In skillet, heat oil over medium-high heat; brown chicken on all sides, about 10 minutes. Transfer to plate and set aside.

• Reduce heat to medium; cook onion, stirring occasionally, for about 5 minutes or until softened. Add mushrooms; cook, stirring occasionally, for 10 minutes or until tender. Add apple juice and vinegar, stirring to scrape up any brown bits; bring to boil.

• Return chicken to pan and bring to boil; reduce heat, cover and simmer for 15 minutes. Uncover and cook for about 5 minutes or until juices run clear when chicken is pierced. Season with salt; sprinkle with parsley.

Makes 4 servings.
PER SERVING: about 250 calories, 29 g protein, 9 g fat, 13 g carbohydrate, good source iron.

Lemon Pepper Chicken and Barbecue-Baked Sage Potatoes

Oregano Sirloin Steak

For the photo, we doubled the amount of steak because a thick 2-lb (1 kg) steak is more often available. Cooking double has its advantages, though. Leftover grilled steak is superb slathered with mustard and tucked into crusty buns.

1 lb	sirloin steak, 1 inch (2.5 cm) thick	500 g
2 tsp	dried oregano (or 2 tbsp/25 mL chopped fresh)	10 mL
2 tsp	olive oil	10 mL
1 tsp	cracked black peppercorns	5 mL
½ tsp	coarse salt	2 mL

- Slash fat around steak at 1-inch (2.5 cm) intervals. Combine oregano, oil, pepper and salt; rub over both sides of steak.

- Place steak on greased grill over medium-high heat; cover and cook, turning once, for about 15 minutes for medium-rare or to desired doneness.

- Transfer to cutting board; tent with foil and let stand for 5 minutes before cutting into portions.

Makes 4 servings.

PER SERVING: about 140 calories, 18 g protein, 6 g fat, 1 g carbohydrate, good source iron.

Herbed Wine Marinated Party Steak

A thick slice of chuck or blade steak is perfect for summer entertaining. The wine-and-vinegar marinade ensures tasty tender fare.

1½ lb	chuck or blade steak, 1 inch (2.5 cm) thick	750 g
¼ cup	red wine	50 mL
3 tbsp	balsamic or red wine vinegar	50 mL
1 tbsp	vegetable oil	15 mL
1 tbsp	Dijon mustard	15 mL
2	cloves garlic, minced	2
1 tbsp	each chopped fresh thyme and oregano (or 1 tsp/5 mL dried)	15 mL
¼ tsp	pepper	1 mL
Pinch	granulated sugar	Pinch

- Place steak in shallow dish. Whisk together wine, vinegar, oil, mustard, garlic, thyme, oregano, pepper and sugar; pour over meat and turn to coat well. Cover and marinate in refrigerator for at least 8 hours or up to 12 hours. Let stand at room temperature for 30 minutes.

- Place steak on greased grill over medium heat; cover and cook, turning twice, for 20 to 30 minutes or until medium-rare. Transfer to cutting board; tent with foil and let stand for 10 minutes before cutting into portions.

Makes 4 servings.
PER SERVING: about 165 calories, 24 g protein, 7 g fat, 1 g carbohydrate, good source iron.

GREAT STEAKS

- Thicker, less tender steaks, such as blade, chuck and inside or bottom round, need marinating. Smaller, more tender steaks, such as tenderloin, sirloin, T-bone and flank, can go directly on the grill.

- Refrain from adding salt to marinades for steaks because salt tends to draw the juices out of meat. Let guests salt their own portions.

- Always let a steak rest for 5 to 10 minutes before carving. This allows the juices to spread from the centre throughout the meat. Carving the meat immediately releases the juices too quickly and the meat will be dry.

Veggie Brochettes

A skewer of vegetables is always right for a barbecue, no matter what's on the grill.

2 tbsp	chopped fresh mint (or 2 tsp/10 mL dried)	25 mL
2 tbsp	each olive oil and lemon juice	25 mL
¼ tsp	ground cumin	1 mL
1	clove garlic, minced	1
1	large zucchini	1
1	large sweet red or yellow pepper	1
1	small red onion	1
Pinch	each salt and pepper	Pinch

- In small bowl, whisk together mint, oil, lemon juice, cumin and garlic; set aside.

- Cut zucchini, red pepper and onion into 1-inch (2.5 cm) chunks; thread onto eight 8-inch (20 cm) soaked wooden skewers.

- Place on greased grill over medium-high heat; cover and cook, turning and basting often with sauce, for about 15 minutes or until tender. Season with salt and pepper.

Makes 4 servings.
PER SERVING: about 70 calories, 1 g protein, 4 g fat, 9 g carbohydrate.

Herb-Baked Tomatoes

Quick-roasting suits busy schedules, but you can also slow-roast plum tomato halves at 300°F (150°C)
until wrinkled (about 2 hours).

6	plum tomatoes	6
1 tbsp	extra-virgin olive oil	15 mL
¼ tsp	each salt and pepper	1 mL
1 tbsp	chopped fresh thyme	15 mL

- Halve tomatoes lengthwise and place on baking sheet; brush with oil. Bake in 450°F (230°C) oven for 15 to 20 minutes or until tender. Season with salt and pepper; sprinkle with thyme.

Makes 6 servings.
PER SERVING: about 35 calories, 1 g protein, 2 g fat, 3 g carbohydrate.

Roasted Asparagus

Roasting highlights the spring-fresh flavor of asparagus. A little seasoning and zippy cheese make it irresistible.

2 lb	asparagus	1 kg
1 tbsp	olive oil	15 mL
½ tsp	pepper	2 mL
¼ tsp	salt	1 mL
2 oz	Asiago or Parmesan cheese	50 g

- Holding asparagus by stem end and halfway up stalk, bend stalk to snap off woody end. In 9-inch (2.5 L) square cake pan, gently toss asparagus with oil, pepper and salt; spread out evenly in pan. Bake in 400°F (200°C) oven for 15 minutes.
- Meanwhile, using vegetable peeler or cheese plane, cut cheese into thin slices. Arrange over asparagus; bake for 2 to 5 minutes or until asparagus is tender-crisp.

Makes 4 to 6 servings.
PER EACH OF 6 SERVINGS: about 79 calories, 5 g protein, 5 g fat, 5 g carbohydrate.

Barbecue-Baked Sage Potatoes

Let sage out! For too long it escaped from the herb bottle only when turkey and chicken were on the menu.
It's fabulous with potatoes and pork as well (see photo page 101).

4	baking potatoes	4
1	sweet red pepper	1
16	sage leaves	16
3 tbsp	olive oil	50 mL
2	cloves garlic, minced	2
½ tsp	each salt and pepper	2 mL

- Scrub potatoes; slice almost through at ¼-inch (5 mm) intervals. Cut red pepper into quarters; slice crosswise into strips. Insert 1 red pepper strip into each slit of potato. Insert sage leaf into every third slit.
- Stir together oil, garlic, salt and pepper; brush over potatoes and red pepper to coat evenly. Wrap each in foil, sealing well.
- Place on grill over medium heat; cover and cook, turning occasionally, for 1 hour or until tender.

Makes 4 servings.
PER SERVING: about 255 calories, 4 g protein, 10 g fat, 38 g carbohydrate, good source iron.

TIP: For cold-weather enjoyment, bake wrapped potatoes in 400°F (200°C) oven for about 45 minutes.

Sesame Chive Tortilla Triangles

A sprinkle of sesame seeds adds a nutty flavor to this crisp flatbread.

6	10-inch (25 cm) flour tortillas	6
1	egg white	1
2 tbsp	sesame oil	25 mL
¼ tsp	salt	1 mL
¼ cup	chopped chives or green onions	50 mL
3 tbsp	sesame seeds, toasted	50 mL

- Arrange 3 of the tortillas on work surface. Lightly beat together egg white, 1 tbsp (15 mL) of the oil and salt; brush over both sides of tortillas.

- Sprinkle with chives and 2 tbsp (25 mL) of the sesame seeds. Top with remaining tortillas, pressing together firmly. Brush remaining oil over top; sprinkle with remaining sesame seeds.

- Arrange in single layer on baking sheet; bake in 400°F (200°C) oven for 10 minutes or until lightly browned. Cut each into 6 wedges and serve warm.

Makes 6 servings.
PER SERVING: about 250 calories, 6 g protein, 10 g fat, 34 g carbohydrate, good source iron.

Layered Black Bean Dip

Simple toppings add a creative touch to this healthy dip. Serve with pita or tortilla crisps.

1	can (14 oz/398 mL) black beans, drained and rinsed	1
½ cup	medium salsa	125 mL
2 tbsp	lime juice	25 mL
¼ tsp	each ground cumin and coriander	1 mL
¼ tsp	each salt and pepper	1 mL
3	green onions, chopped	3
Half	each sweet green and red pepper, diced	Half
1 tbsp	light sour cream	15 mL
1 tbsp	chopped fresh coriander or parsley	15 mL

- In food processor, purée together beans, salsa, lime juice, cumin, coriander, salt and pepper; spread in small serving bowl.

- Top dip evenly with green onions. Scatter green pepper around edge of bowl. Arrange red pepper in centre; dollop with sour cream. Sprinkle with fresh coriander.

Makes about 2 cups (500 mL).
PER 2 TBSP (25 mL): about 30 calories, 2 g protein, trace fat, 6 g carbohydrate.

> TIP: Black beans are often easier to find dry than canned. Since beans are so effortless to cook, here's how to prepare them for this dip. Cover ⅔ cup (150 mL) dry black beans with 2 cups (500 mL) cold water. Either soak overnight or bring to boil for 2 minutes. Cover and let stand for 1 hour. Drain, cover again, this time with 4 cups (1 L) cold water; boil, covered, until tender, about 1 hour. Yield is about 1⅓ cups (325 mL), a touch less than the yield of a 14-oz (398 mL) can.

Zesty Quesadilla Bites

Once you get the hang of layering tortillas over favorite fillers, you won't need a recipe.

6	8-inch (20 cm) flour tortillas	6
1 cup	shredded Monterey Jack cheese	250 mL
¼ cup	diced green chilies	50 mL
¾ cup	chopped roasted sweet red peppers	175 mL
¾ cup	cooked corn kernels (optional)	175 mL

- Place 3 tortillas in single layer on work surface, or on large baking sheet if baking in oven. Sprinkle cheese evenly over tortillas. Sprinkle with chilies; top with red peppers, and corn (if using).

- Moisten edge of each covered tortilla with water; top with remaining tortilla, pressing edges to seal.

- Place on lightly greased grill over medium heat; cover and cook for 5 to 8 minutes, or bake in 375°F (190°C) oven for 8 to 10 minutes, turning once, or until browned, crisped and cheese is melted. To serve, cut into wedges.

Makes 4 to 6 servings.

PER EACH OF 6 SERVINGS: about 215 calories, 8 g protein, 8 g fat, 26 g carbohydrate, good source calcium.

Tahini Dip

Tahini, ground sesame seed paste, is a major player in Middle Eastern flavors (it's what gives hummus its nutty taste). Serve with toasted pita triangles, carrots, celery and sweet pepper sticks.

1 cup	tahini	250 mL
1 tsp	finely grated lemon rind	5 mL
⅓ cup	lemon juice	75 mL
3 tbsp	chopped fresh parsley	50 mL
3	cloves garlic, minced	3
¾ tsp	ground cumin	4 mL
¾ tsp	salt	4 mL

- In bowl, stir ⅓ cup (75 mL) water into tahini. Stir in lemon rind and juice, then another ⅓ cup (75 mL) water.

- Stir in parsley, garlic, cumin and salt. *(Dip can be covered and refrigerated for up to 8 hours. Serve at room temperature.)*

Makes about 2 cups (500 mL).

PER 2 TBSP (25 mL): about 90 calories, 3 g protein, 8 g fat, 3 g carbohydrate.

Strawberry-Glazed Brie

Surround this gooey warm cheese with crackers to scoop up all the tangy goodness.

¾ cup	strawberries, mashed	175 mL
4 tsp	packed brown sugar	20 mL
2 tsp	lemon juice	10 mL
Pinch	cinnamon	Pinch
2	rounds (each 4 oz/125 g) Brie cheese	2

TIP: You can use an 8-oz (250 g) wedge of cheese instead of the rounds.

- In small saucepan, combine strawberries, sugar, lemon juice and cinnamon; bring to boil. Reduce heat and simmer for about 6 minutes or until thickened; let cool slightly.

- Remove rind from top of Brie; place on ovenproof platter. Spread strawberry mixture evenly over top; bake in 300°F (150°C) oven for about 12 minutes or until cheese is softened but not melted.

Makes 8 servings.

PER SERVING: about 110 calories, 6 g protein, 8 g fat, 3 g carbohydrate.

Devilled Egg Trio

This perennial picnic favorite from chef Dana McCauley is back with a new, lighter twist and two additional flavor choices — curried and toasted almond.

6	hard-cooked eggs	6
¼ cup	light mayonnaise	50 mL
2 tsp	finely chopped fresh dill	10 mL
2 tsp	chopped capers	10 mL
1 tsp	sweet mustard	5 mL
¼ tsp	pepper	1 mL
	Salt	
	Paprika	
12	sprigs fresh dill	12

TIP: To avoid a green ring around yolks of hard-cooked eggs, place eggs in saucepan with just enough cold water to cover; bring to boil. Cover pan and remove from heat; let stand for 20 minutes. Drain and chill under cold water; peel off shells.

- Halve eggs lengthwise; carefully scoop out yolks. In bowl, mash yolks with mayonnaise. Stir in chopped dill, capers, mustard, pepper, and salt to taste.

- Using piping bag or spoon, pipe filling into cavities of egg whites. Sprinkle lightly with paprika; garnish with sprig of dill.

   Makes 6 servings.
   PER SERVING: about 110 calories, 6 g protein, 8 g fat, 2 g carbohydrate.

VARIATIONS
- CURRIED DEVILLED EGGS: Omit dill, capers, mustard and paprika. Stir 1 tsp (5 mL) minced onion and ½ tsp (2 mL) curry powder into mashed egg yolks. Garnish with dab of chutney and sprig of fresh coriander.
- ALMOND DEVILLED EGGS: Omit dill, capers, mustard and paprika. Stir 1 tsp (5 mL) chopped fresh parsley, ½ tsp (2 mL) grainy mustard and dash of Worcestershire sauce into mashed egg yolk. Garnish with chopped toasted almond.

Grilled Zucchini Salad

Zucchini and the barbecue — a combination made in food heaven. Here's how to get rid of that pesky summer squash and love every bite.

4	zucchini (1 lb/500 g total)	4
¾ tsp	salt	4 mL
2 tbsp	olive oil	25 mL
1 tsp	dried thyme	5 mL
¼ tsp	pepper	1 mL
4 tsp	red wine vinegar or lemon juice	20 mL
1	small clove garlic, minced (optional)	1
2 tsp	chopped fresh oregano (or ½ tsp/2 mL dried) or two chive flowers, pulled apart	10 mL

TIP: Bring chilled marinated vegetable salads to room temperature before serving.

- Cut each zucchini lengthwise into 4 slices about ¼ inch (5 mm) thick. Place in colander; sprinkle with salt and let drain for at least 30 minutes or up to 2 hours. Rinse well under cold water; drain and pat dry.

- In bowl, toss zucchini with oil, thyme and pepper until evenly coated. Place on greased grill over medium heat; cover and cook, turning once, for about 7 minutes or until tender and limp.

- Toss warm zucchini with vinegar, and garlic (if using); arrange in overlapping layers in shallow dish. Let cool. *(Salad can be covered and refrigerated for up to 1 day.)* Garnish with oregano.

   Makes 4 servings.
   PER SERVING: about 80 calories, 1 g protein, 7 g fat, 4 g carbohydrate.

Grilled Chicken Caesar Salad

We've lightened up this usually high-fat salad and made it a main course with grilled chicken breasts.

4	boneless skinless chicken breasts	4
8 cups	shredded lettuce	2 L
¼ cup	slivered sun-dried tomatoes	50 mL
DRESSING:		
1 tbsp	red wine vinegar	15 mL
1 tbsp	chicken stock	15 mL
1	clove garlic, minced	1
½ tsp	Dijon mustard	2 mL
¼ tsp	anchovy paste	1 mL
¼ cup	olive oil	50 mL
1 tbsp	freshly grated Parmesan cheese	15 mL
¼ tsp	pepper	1 mL

TIP: To make this salad year-round, bake chicken on baking sheet in 375°F (190°C) oven for 20 minutes.

- DRESSING: In bowl, whisk together vinegar, stock, garlic, mustard and anchovy paste; gradually whisk in oil. Stir in Parmesan cheese and pepper.

- In shallow glass bowl, pour 2 tbsp (25 mL) of the dressing over chicken, turning to coat. Let stand for 20 minutes.

- Place chicken on greased grill over medium-high heat; cover and cook, turning once, for about 8 minutes or until no longer pink. Transfer to cutting board; tent with foil and let stand for 10 minutes. Cut into slices.

- Reserve 2 tbsp (25 mL) of the dressing. Toss lettuce with remaining dressing; divide among plates. Arrange chicken over lettuce; spoon reserved dressing over chicken. Sprinkle with tomatoes.

Makes 4 servings.
PER SERVING: about 290 calories, 30 g protein, 16 g fat, 6 g carbohydrate, good source iron.

Anne Lindsay's Ranch-Style Buttermilk Dressing

This has been a signature dressing in the Lindsay house for more than a decade. No doubt its good taste and healthful ingredients will keep Anne whisking it up for years to come.

1 cup	buttermilk	250 mL
⅓ cup	light mayonnaise	75 mL
1	small clove garlic, minced	1
2 tbsp	chopped fresh parsley	25 mL
½ tsp	granulated sugar	2 mL
½ tsp	dried dillweed	2 mL
¼ tsp	dry mustard	1 mL
Pinch	pepper	Pinch

- In small bowl or jar, combine buttermilk, mayonnaise, garlic, parsley, sugar, dillweed, mustard and pepper; mix well. Cover and refrigerate for up to 4 days.

Makes 1⅓ cups (325 mL).
PER 2 TBSP (25 mL): about 35 calories, 1 g protein, 2 g fat, 2 g carbohydrate.

Exotic Green Salad

A sense of intrigue highlights this refreshing dressing for radicchio and Belgian endive.

2	Belgian endives	2
1	head radicchio or ruby lettuce	1
1	head Boston lettuce	1
DRESSING:		
2 tbsp	balsamic vinegar	25 mL
1 tbsp	soy sauce	15 mL
1 tbsp	lemon juice	15 mL
2 tsp	liquid honey	10 mL
½ tsp	minced gingerroot	2 mL
½ tsp	salt	2 mL
¼ tsp	pepper	1 mL
1	clove garlic, minced	1
¼ cup	olive oil	50 mL
2 tbsp	each chopped fresh coriander and basil	25 mL

- DRESSING: In bowl, whisk together vinegar, soy sauce, lemon juice, honey, ginger, salt, pepper and garlic; gradually whisk in oil. Stir in coriander and basil.

- Trim endives; separate into leaves. Separate and tear radicchio and Boston lettuce into bite-size pieces. In salad bowl, toss greens with dressing.

Makes 6 servings.
PER SERVING: about 105 calories, 1 g protein, 9 g fat, 5 g carbohydrate.

Asparagus Salad

Some Canadians count on robins as the first sign of spring. But when home-grown asparagus appears, others know spring has truly sprung one of its best treasures.

1	hard-cooked egg	1
2 tbsp	lemon juice	25 mL
1 tbsp	balsamic vinegar	15 mL
2 tsp	Dijon mustard	10 mL
1	clove garlic, minced	1
¼ tsp	each salt and pepper	1 mL
⅓ cup	olive oil	75 mL
2 lb	asparagus, trimmed	1 kg
	Red leaf or other lettuce	
9	cherry tomatoes, halved	9

- Halve egg and scoop out yolk; chop white and refrigerate. In bowl, mash yolk into paste; whisk in lemon juice, vinegar, mustard, garlic, salt and pepper. Gradually whisk in oil. (*Dressing can be covered and refrigerated for up to 24 hours; let stand at room temperature for 30 minutes. Whisk again.*)

- In shallow saucepan of boiling water, cook asparagus for 3 minutes or just until tender-crisp; drain. (*Asparagus can be wrapped in towel and set aside for up to 3 hours.*)

- Line serving platter with lettuce; top with asparagus. Spoon dressing over asparagus; sprinkle with egg white. Garnish with tomatoes.

Makes 6 servings.
PER SERVING: about 155 calories, 4 g protein, 13 g fat, 6 g carbohydrate.

Grilled Shrimp and Mushroom Salad

Make this warm and light salad year-round by broiling the shrimp.

16	large raw shrimp, peeled and deveined (tails left on)	16
16	small mushrooms	16
6 cups	fresh spinach	1.5 L
1	small bunch watercress	1
1	small head radicchio lettuce	1
DRESSING:		
¼ cup	tarragon vinegar	50 mL
¼ cup	lemon juice	50 mL
2 tbsp	olive oil	25 mL
1 tsp	Dijon mustard	5 mL
¼ tsp	each salt and pepper	1 mL
2	cloves garlic, minced	2
2 tbsp	minced shallots or green onions	25 mL

TIP: To keep shrimp firmly on skewers, pierce each through top end and tail end when threading.

- **DRESSING:** In small saucepan, whisk together vinegar, lemon juice, oil, mustard, salt and pepper; stir in garlic and shallots.

- In bowl, combine shrimp, mushrooms and 2 tbsp (25 mL) of the dressing; stir gently to coat. Let stand for 15 minutes.

- Meanwhile, tear spinach, watercress and radicchio into bite-size pieces; place in large bowl.

- Thread shrimp and mushrooms onto separate skewers. Place on greased grill over medium heat; cover and cook, turning once, for about 5 minutes or just until shrimp are pink and mushrooms are lightly browned.

- Meanwhile, bring reserved dressing just to boil; pour half over greens and toss to coat. Divide among plates.

- Push shrimp and mushrooms off skewers onto greens. Drizzle with remaining dressing. Serve warm.

Makes 4 servings.
PER SERVING: about 225 calories, 26 g protein, 9 g fat, 11 g carbohydrate, high source fibre, excellent source iron.

Grilled Sweet Pepper Salad

This salad is perfect for a stylish summer lunch. Just add a sunny porch, a loaf of crusty bread and a few shavings of a cheese with personality, such as Asiago.

6	sweet red or green peppers	6
⅔ cup	shredded fresh basil	150 mL
⅓ cup	sliced green onions	75 mL
3 tbsp	olive oil	50 mL
1 tbsp	red wine vinegar	15 mL
1	large clove garlic, minced	1
½ tsp	salt	2 mL
¼ tsp	pepper	1 mL

- On baking sheet, broil peppers, turning occasionally, for about 20 minutes or until blistered and charred all over. Transfer to large bowl; cover and let steam for 20 minutes. Set sieve over large bowl; peel, core and seed peppers over sieve, reserving ¼ cup (50 mL) pepper liquid. Cut peppers in half.

- In small bowl, whisk together basil, onions, oil, vinegar, reserved pepper liquid, garlic, salt and pepper. Using fork, lift about 1 heaping teaspoonful (5 mL) of the basil mixture out of dressing; spread inside half of each pepper. Fold other half over and arrange, overlapping, in single layer in shallow serving dish.

- Drizzle with remaining dressing; cover and refrigerate for at least 4 hours or up to 24 hours. Let come to room temperature before serving.

Makes 6 servings.
PER SERVING: about 100 calories, 1 g protein, 7 g fat, 9 g carbohydrate.

Roseville Tea Sandwiches

Long-time Canadian Living *photographer Frank Grant returned to his native Australia recently and renewed his love for Roseville, a historic house in Brisbane in the semi-tropical part of Queensland. Tea is a specialty; the garden, an invitation to relax.*

¼ cup	mayonnaise	50 mL
1 tbsp	minced green onion	15 mL
1 tbsp	each chopped fresh dill and capers	15 mL
1 ½ tsp	prepared horseradish	7 mL
Pinch	pepper	Pinch
8	slices whole wheat bread	8
1 ½ tsp	butter, softened	7 mL
4	slices smoked salmon	4
12	thin slices cucumber	12

- In small bowl, combine mayonnaise, onion, dill, capers, horseradish and pepper. Trim crusts from bread; spread with butter, then mayonnaise mixture.

- Arrange salmon and cucumber over 4 of the bread slices; top with remaining bread. Cut each sandwich into 4 triangles or squares.

Makes 4 servings.
PER SERVING: about 250 calories, 8 g protein, 15 g fat, 23 g carbohydrate.

THAT PERFECT CUP OF TEA

Put a teakettle of fresh cold water on to boil. Count on 6 oz (175 mL) per cup. Meanwhile, warm teapot with some boiling water; swirl and drain. Add tea: for each cup either 1 bag or 1 heaping tsp (5 mL) loose leaves and an extra spoonful for the pot. It makes cleaning out the pot a lot easier if you place the loose tea in an infuser. As soon as kettle comes to boil, pour water over tea; replace teapot lid, cover with cosy if desired and let steep for 4 to 6 minutes. Remove bags or infuser.
Black teas such as orange pekoe, Darjeeling, English Breakfast and lapsang souchong are recommended, as is Earl Grey, the black tea scented with oil of bergamot.

CHAPTER SIX

ALL DRESSED UP

When the guest list, the occasion and the excitement of the event all demand a pull-out-the-stops kind of spread, here are the dishes that will help you succeed in a calm and organized fashion. You'll be proud and your guests will not only be pleased but impressed to boot.

Savory Herb Cheesecake

Serve thin wedges of this easy-to-make cheesecake warm over a bed of dressed salad greens. It's a great dish for lunch or as a first course at a dinner party.

1½ cups	fresh bread crumbs	375 mL
⅔ cup	finely chopped walnuts	150 mL
3 tbsp	butter, softened	50 mL
1¼ lb	cream cheese, at room temperature	625 g
¼ cup	freshly grated Parmesan cheese	50 mL
4	eggs	4
2	cloves garlic, minced	2
2 tbsp	each chopped fresh tarragon, basil and oregano	25 mL
¼ tsp	pepper	1 mL

- In food processor, combine bread crumbs, walnuts and butter until well mixed. Press onto bottom of 8-inch (2 L) springform pan. Bake in 350°F (180°C) oven for 15 minutes or until golden.

- Meanwhile, in bowl and using hand mixer, beat together cream cheese and Parmesan cheese until smooth; beat in eggs, 1 at a time, beating well after each addition. Stir in garlic, tarragon, basil, oregano and pepper; pour over base. Bake for about 1 hour or until golden and puffed.

- Run sharp knife around edge of cake; let stand for 15 minutes before carefully removing side of pan. (Cake will fall slightly upon cooling.) Cut into wedges.

Makes 12 appetizers.
PER APPETIZER: about 290 calories, 8 g protein, 26 g fat, 6 g carbohydrate.

HERB APPEAL

- If fresh herbs are unavailable, substitute one-third to one-half the amount of dried for fresh.

- Wash and dry fresh-cut herbs and store in airtight container in the refrigerator for up to 2 weeks. Store dried herbs away from air, heat and light, and for no longer than 1 year.

- Before adding a dried herb to a recipe, rub leaves between your fingers to release flavor.

- Whole-leaf dried herbs are better than ground because they stay fresh longer.

Thai Grilled Shrimp

Shrimp says special, and with this subtly spiced marinade, it is positively irresistible at a party.

1 ¼ lb	raw shrimp (about 40)	625 g
½ cup	chopped onion	125 mL
3 tbsp	vegetable oil	50 mL
1 tbsp	ground coriander	15 mL
1 tbsp	grated lemon rind	15 mL
1 tbsp	lemon juice	15 mL
1 tbsp	Thai fish sauce or soy sauce	15 mL
1 tsp	chili powder	5 mL
½ tsp	minced garlic	2 mL
¼ tsp	hot pepper sauce	1 mL
1 tbsp	chopped fresh parsley	15 mL

- Peel and devein shrimp, leaving tails on; place in bowl.

- In blender, purée together onion, oil, coriander, lemon rind and juice, fish sauce, chili powder, garlic and hot pepper sauce; pour over shrimp. Add parsley and toss to coat. Cover and refrigerate for 1 hour.

- Reserving marinade, thread 2 shrimp onto each soaked wooden skewer. Place on greased grill over medium-high heat; cover and cook, turning once and brushing with marinade, for 4 minutes or until pink. (Or broil for 2 to 3 minutes.)

Makes 20 hors d'oeuvres.
PER HORS D'OEUVRE: about 45 calories, 5 g protein, 2 g fat, 1 g carbohydrate.

TIP: Thai fish sauce is available in many Asian grocery stores. It is made from fermented fish, so don't let your first whiff put you off. It mellows and blends with other flavors and adds an authenticity to this dish.

Samosa Potato Cups

Samosas are deep-fried savory pastries with various fillings. We've rescued this delicious morsel from the deep-fryer and made it easier to make using phyllo pastry.

4	sheets phyllo pastry	4
¼ cup	butter, melted	50 mL
FILLING:		
1 tsp	cumin seeds	5 mL
2 tsp	butter	10 mL
1	small onion, diced	1
½ tsp	minced gingerroot	2 mL
¼ tsp	salt	1 mL
Pinch	each cayenne and turmeric	Pinch
1 cup	finely diced peeled potatoes	250 mL
¼ cup	frozen green peas	50 mL
¼ cup	plain yogurt	50 mL
	Diced sweet red pepper	

TIP: The empty phyllo cups can be stored at room temperature for up to 3 days, and the filling can be refrigerated for up to 1 day — each in an individual airtight container.

- Place 1 sheet of phyllo on work surface, covering remaining phyllo with damp towel to prevent drying out. Brush with butter. Top with second sheet; brush with butter. Repeat with remaining phyllo.

- Cut phyllo into 2-inch (5 cm) squares; place in greased 1¾-inch (4.5 cm) mini tart tins. Bake in 350°F (180°C) oven for 10 minutes or until golden. Let cool.

- FILLING: In skillet, toast cumin seeds over medium-high heat for 30 seconds; remove and set aside.

- Melt butter in skillet over medium heat; cook onion, ginger, salt, cayenne, turmeric and cumin seeds, stirring, for 3 minutes or until onion is softened.

- Add potatoes and ⅓ cup (75 mL) water; cover and cook, stirring occasionally, for 10 to 15 minutes or until potatoes are tender and water is absorbed. Stir in peas; cook for 2 minutes. Let cool.

- Stir yogurt into filling; spoon 1 tsp (5 mL) into each phyllo cup. Garnish with red pepper.

Makes 48 hors d'oeuvres.
PER HORS D'OEUVRE: about 20 calories, trace protein, 1 g fat, 2 g carbohydrate.

Mushroom, Fennel and Parmesan Salad

Here's where real Parmesan, Parmigiano-Reggiano, is a must. The combination of its nuttiness, fennel's crisp licorice taste and the woodsy mushrooms is good to the last sliver.

1	bulb fennel	1
¼ lb	chunk Parmesan cheese	125 g
4 cups	thinly sliced mushrooms (¾ lb/375 g)	1 L
2 tbsp	each chopped fresh parsley and basil	25 mL
8	leaves each radicchio and Boston lettuce	8
DRESSING:		
2 tbsp	red wine vinegar	25 mL
2 tbsp	balsamic vinegar	25 mL
½ tsp	each salt and pepper	2 mL
⅓ cup	olive oil	75 mL

- Trim fennel; slice as thinly as possible. Trim Parmesan of rind or dry crust. With cheese plane or knife, slice cheese as thinly as possible; set 8 slices aside for garnish.

- In large bowl, combine fennel, remaining cheese, mushrooms, parsley and basil. *(Salad can be prepared to this point, covered and refrigerated for up to 12 hours.)*

- DRESSING: In small bowl, whisk together red wine and balsamic vinegars, salt and pepper; gradually whisk in oil. *(Dressing can be covered and set aside for up to 12 hours.)* Toss with salad to coat.

- Form 1 leaf each radicchio and Boston lettuce into cup on each plate; spoon in salad. Garnish with reserved cheese slices.

Makes 8 servings.
PER SERVING: about 165 calories, 7 g protein, 14 g fat, 5 g carbohydrate, good source calcium.

Curried Lentil, Wild Rice and Orzo Salad

Don't let the length of the ingredient list put you off. This sweetly spiced grain salad is one recipe guests always want.

½ cup	wild rice	125 mL
⅔ cup	green or brown lentils	150 mL
½ cup	orzo pasta	125 mL
½ cup	currants	125 mL
¼ cup	finely chopped red onion	50 mL
⅓ cup	slivered almonds, toasted	75 mL
DRESSING:		
¼ cup	white wine vinegar	50 mL
1 tsp	ground cumin	5 mL
1 tsp	Dijon mustard	5 mL
½ tsp	each granulated sugar, salt and ground coriander	2 mL
¼ tsp	each turmeric, paprika, nutmeg and ground cardamom	1 mL
Pinch	each cinnamon, cloves and cayenne	Pinch
⅓ cup	vegetable oil	75 mL

- In large pot of boiling salted water, cook wild rice, covered, for 10 minutes. Add lentils; boil for 20 minutes. Add orzo; boil for about 5 minutes or just until tender. Drain well and transfer to large bowl. Add currants and onion; set aside.

- DRESSING: In small bowl, whisk together vinegar, cumin, mustard, sugar, salt, coriander, turmeric, paprika, nutmeg, cardamom, cinnamon, cloves and cayenne; whisk in oil. Pour over rice mixture and toss gently.

- Let salad cool completely; cover and refrigerate for at least 4 hours or up to 2 days. Just before serving, sprinkle with almonds.

Makes 6 servings.
PER SERVING: about 365 calories, 11 g protein, 17 g fat, 45 g carbohydrate, high source fibre, excellent source iron.

> TIP: If you like, you can cook the rice, lentils and orzo separately, so it's a little easier to monitor doneness.

Coriander Chili Dip

Coriander or cilantro (English and Spanish, respectively) is the herb that's so popular in Latin American, Indian and Southeast Asian cooking. Partner this zesty dip with crunchy vegetables.

1 cup	plain yogurt	250 mL
1 cup	sour cream	250 mL
⅓ cup	chopped fresh coriander	75 mL
1 tsp	minced hot green chili or jalapeño pepper	5 mL
¾ tsp	pepper	4 mL
½ tsp	salt	2 mL

- In small bowl, combine yogurt, sour cream, coriander, chili pepper, pepper and salt. Cover and refrigerate for 4 hours or up to 24 hours.

Makes 2 cups (500 mL).
PER 2 TBSP (25 mL): about 35 calories, 1 g protein, 2 g fat, 2 g carbohydrate.

Antipasto Salad

Whether it's an appetizer, picnic platter or light supper, this colorful array of vegetables, cheese and cold cuts is as versatile as it is varied.

2	zucchini, cubed	2
1	sweet yellow or green pepper, chopped	1
Quarter	small white or Spanish onion, sliced in half-moons	Quarter
1 cup	cooked white pea beans	250 mL
⅓ cup	oil-cured black olives, pitted	75 mL
1 cup	cubed Asiago, provolone or mozzarella cheese (about 6 oz/175 g)	250 mL
¼ lb	sliced capocollo or other ham, cubed	125 g
½ cup	chopped fresh basil	125 mL
¼ cup	chopped fresh parsley	50 mL
4	plum tomatoes	4
8	leaves romaine lettuce	8
DRESSING:		
⅓ cup	olive oil	75 mL
¼ cup	balsamic or red wine vinegar	50 mL
½ tsp	salt	2 mL
¼ tsp	pepper	1 mL
2	cloves garlic, minced	2

- DRESSING: In large bowl, whisk together oil, vinegar, salt, pepper and garlic. Add zucchini, yellow pepper, onion, beans, olives, Asiago cheese, capocollo, half of the basil and half of the parsley; toss gently to combine. *(Salad can be prepared to this point, covered and refrigerated for up to 8 hours.)*

- Core tomatoes; cut into 8 wedges. Line shallow bowl with lettuce; mound salad on top. Garnish with tomatoes and remaining basil and parsley.

Makes 6 servings.

PER SERVING: about 340 calories, 16 g protein, 24 g fat, 17 g carbohydrate, high source fibre, excellent source calcium.

> TIP: Though the uncooked zucchini is just fine, if you have time, replace it with grilled zucchini cut into bite-size pieces.

Warm Lobster Dip

Surrounded with crackers, this rich-tasting dip, a specialty of Nova Scotian Dr. Clair MacLeod, is so delicious, you'll find it impossible to stop at just a few bites.

1	can (5 oz/142 g) lobster	1
½ lb	light cream cheese, cubed	250 g
¼ cup	Sauterne or other white wine	50 mL
1 tbsp	light mayonnaise	15 mL
1	clove garlic, minced	1
1 tsp	finely chopped onion	5 mL
1 tsp	granulated sugar	5 mL
1 tsp	Dijon mustard	5 mL
Pinch	each salt and cayenne pepper	Pinch

- Drain lobster; flake meat with fingers and set aside.

- In small saucepan, melt cheese over low heat until smooth, stirring often. Stir in lobster, wine, mayonnaise, garlic, onion, sugar, mustard, salt and cayenne; heat through, stirring occasionally. Serve in warmed bowl.

Makes about 2 cups (500 mL).

PER 1 TBSP (15 mL): about 30 calories, 1 g protein, 2 g fat, 1 g carbohydrate.

VARIATION

- CRAB DIP: Substitute 1 pkg (7 oz/200 g) frozen crab for the lobster.

Grilled Thai Beef Salad

No wonder Thai food is all the rage these days. With its range of textures, from tender to crisp, its friendly Asian flavor accents have enormous taste appeal.

¾ lb	flank steak	375 g
2 tbsp	fish sauce	25 mL
2 tbsp	lime juice	25 mL
2 tbsp	hoisin sauce	25 mL
4 tsp	minced gingerroot	20 mL
1 tbsp	sherry	15 mL
1	clove garlic, minced	1
½ tsp	chili paste or hot pepper sauce	2 mL
½ tsp	sesame oil	2 mL
8 cups	torn red-tipped leaf lettuce	2 L
2 cups	snow peas (6 oz/175 g)	500 mL
1	sweet red pepper	1
Half	small English cucumber	Half
1 cup	bean sprouts	250 mL
1 tbsp	balsamic vinegar	15 mL
½ tsp	granulated sugar	2 mL
2 tbsp	olive oil	25 mL

- Place steak in large shallow glass dish. Whisk together fish sauce, lime juice, hoisin sauce, ginger, sherry, garlic, chili paste and sesame oil; pour over meat, turning to coat. Cover and marinate in refrigerator, turning occasionally, for at least 8 hours or up to 24 hours. Let stand at room temperature for 30 minutes.

- Place lettuce in large attractive salad bowl. In small saucepan of boiling water, cook snow peas for 2 minutes or until tender-crisp. Drain and refresh under cold water; drain again, pat dry and add to salad bowl.

- Seed and core red pepper; cut into thin strips and add to bowl. Slice cucumber in half lengthwise; slice thinly crosswise and add to bowl. Add bean sprouts.

- Reserving marinade, place steak on greased grill over medium-high heat; cover and cook, turning once, for about 10 minutes or until medium-rare. Transfer to cutting board and tent with foil; let stand for 5 minutes. Slice diagonally across the grain into thin slices; add to salad bowl.

- Meanwhile, in small saucepan, bring marinade to boil; boil gently for 5 minutes. Remove from heat. Whisk in vinegar and sugar; gradually whisk in olive oil. Let cool slightly. Pour over salad; toss gently until lightly coated.

Makes 4 servings.

PER SERVING: about 300 calories, 25 g protein, 15 g fat, 17 g carbohydrate, high source fibre, excellent source iron.

VARIATIONS

- THAI PORK SALAD: Use pork tenderloin instead of flank steak. Grill, turning once, for 20 to 25 minutes or until just a hint of pink remains inside.
- THAI CHICKEN SALAD: Use 3 boneless skinless chicken breasts instead of flank steak. Grill, turning once, for 8 to 10 minutes or until no longer pink inside.

Pepper Roast Beef

Slow-cooking this lean cut of beef results in a fabulous roast, an update on a good old-fashioned Canadian roast beef dinner.

2 tbsp	peppercorns	25 mL
1 tsp	dried oregano	5 mL
3 lb	inside round roast of beef	1.5 kg
2	cloves garlic, sliced	2
1 tbsp	vegetable oil	15 mL
GRAVY:		
2 tbsp	butter	25 mL
1	small onion, finely chopped	1
2 tbsp	all-purpose flour	25 mL
1 cup	beef stock	250 mL
1 cup	red wine or beef stock	250 mL
Pinch	salt	Pinch

- Between sheets of waxed paper, pound peppercorns with mallet until coarsely crushed. Mix in oregano; spread out evenly.

- Make small slits in roast; insert garlic slice in each. Brush with oil. Roll in peppercorn mixture to coat all over; place on greased rack in roasting pan.

- Roast in 275°F (140°C) oven for 2 hours or until meat thermometer registers 140°F (60°C) for rare or 160°F (70°C) for medium. Transfer to warmed platter; tent with foil and let stand for 15 minutes. Slice thinly.

- GRAVY: Meanwhile, in roasting pan, melt butter over medium heat; cook onion, stirring often, for about 5 minutes or until golden. Stir in flour; cook, stirring, for 1 minute.

- Add beef stock, wine and salt; bring to boil, stirring to scrape up brown bits. Reduce heat and simmer for about 2 minutes or until thickened. Strain into sauceboat; pass with meat.

Makes 8 servings.
PER SERVING: about 375 calories, 38 g protein, 20 g fat, 4 g carbohydrate, excellent source iron.

TIP: Today's medium-tender cuts of beef are best cooked only to rare or medium. Slow-roasting at 275°F (140°C) for 40 minutes per pound (90 minutes per kilogram) ensures juicy results. However, a rolled, tied roast may be thicker, requiring an extra 10 minutes per pound (500 grams).

Red Pepper Glazed Pork Chops

Strips of sweet red pepper and the gloss of hot pepper jelly turn everyday pork chops into a visual and gastronomic event. Serve with rice, preferably an Indian basmati, and crunchy sugar snap peas.

4	pork chops, ¾ inch (2 cm) thick	4
½ tsp	salt	2 mL
¼ tsp	pepper	1 mL
1 tbsp	vegetable oil	15 mL
1	sweet red pepper, thinly sliced	1
1	small onion, finely chopped	1
½ cup	red pepper jelly	125 mL
2 tbsp	cider vinegar	25 mL
¾ tsp	hot pepper sauce	4 mL

- Trim fat from chops; sprinkle all over with salt and pepper. In large nonstick skillet, heat oil over medium-high heat; cook chops for 3 minutes per side or until browned and just a hint of pink remains inside. Transfer to plate and keep warm.

- Add red pepper and onion to pan; cook, stirring occasionally, for about 5 minutes or until softened. Add red pepper jelly, vinegar and hot pepper sauce; reduce heat to medium and cook for about 6 minutes or until thickened.

- Return chops and any juices to pan; cook, turning to coat, for about 2 minutes or until heated through.

Makes 4 servings.
PER SERVING: about 310 calories, 25 g protein, 10 g fat, 30 g carbohydrate.

Sage-Grilled Chicken Halves

Grilling chicken halves takes less time than cooking a whole chicken on the barbecue and makes it easier to serve to guests.

1	chicken (about 3 lb/1.5 kg)	1
3 tbsp	Dijon mustard	50 mL
2 tbsp	freshly grated Parmesan cheese	25 mL
1	small clove garlic, minced	1
8	sage leaves	8
¼ tsp	each salt and pepper	1 mL

- Place chicken, breast side down, on cutting board. Trim off and discard any visible fat at cavity and neck. Using kitchen shears or large chef's knife, cut along both sides of backbone to separate from body; remove and reserve to make stock. Turn chicken over; open up slightly and cut in half through middle of breastbone. Cut off wing tips.

- With fingers and starting at breast end of chicken, gently loosen skin over breast, thigh and as far up drumstick as possible, keeping skin attached to breastbone as much as possible to form pocket.

- Stir together mustard, Parmesan cheese and garlic; spoon half over breast and leg meat, pressing skin to help spread evenly. Ease in 2 sage leaves to cover mustard mixture over leg. Place 2 sage leaves over mustard mixture on breast, pulling skin back over to cover. Repeat with other chicken half. Sprinkle chicken with salt and pepper. Let stand at room temperature for 30 minutes.

- Place chicken, bone side down, on greased grill over medium heat; cover and cook for 10 to 15 minutes or until golden brown. Turn and cook for 15 minutes. Turn and cook for 15 minutes longer or until juices run clear when chicken is pierced. Remove to platter and tent with foil; let stand for 5 minutes before cutting into portions.

Makes 4 servings.
PER SERVING: about 325 calories, 36 g protein, 18 g fat, 1 g carbohydrate.

Margaret Fraser's Barbecued Cornish Hens

Cornish hens are a little something out of the ordinary to serve your guests. Although they are more expensive than chicken, they do taste grand.

2	large blue or red plums (or 6 small prune plums), pitted	2
½ cup	orange juice	125 mL
2 tbsp	packed brown sugar	25 mL
2 tbsp	chili sauce	25 mL
1 tsp	lemon juice	5 mL
	Salt	
¼ tsp	hot pepper sauce	1 mL
4	Cornish hens (about 1 lb/500 g each)	4
	Pepper	
GARNISH:		
	Plum halves and fresh parsley	

TIP: If plums are unavailable, substitute 1 can (14 oz/398 mL) prune plums, drained, pitted and blended with ½ cup (125 mL) reserved juice instead of the orange juice.

- In blender or food processor, combine plums, orange juice, sugar, chili sauce, lemon juice, ½ tsp (2 mL) salt and hot pepper sauce; blend until smooth. Pour into saucepan; bring to boil. Remove from heat; set aside. (Alternatively, microwave at High for 2½ to 3 minutes, stirring twice.)

- Wash hens and pat dry with paper towels. Sprinkle cavities lightly with salt and pepper. Tie legs together; tie wings tightly to body.

- Place hens on greased grill over drip pan; cover and cook over medium-high heat for 20 minutes. Brush with plum mixture; cook, brushing several times with plum mixture, for 20 to 30 minutes longer or until meat is no longer pink near bone.

- Garnish: Arrange hens on platter; garnish with plums and parsley. Heat any remaining sauce; spoon over top.

Makes 4 servings.
PER SERVING: about 605 calories, 61 g protein, 31 g fat, 17 g carbohydrate, good source iron.

Roast Lamb with Tapenade

Tapenade is a Provençal spread made from black olives. Partner it with lamb, rosemary, garlic and Roast Potato Slices (see page 127) for a delicious taste trip to the south of France.

1	butterflied leg of lamb (about 3 lb/1.5 kg)	1
2 tbsp	Dijon mustard	25 mL
1 tbsp	chopped fresh rosemary (or 1 tsp/5 mL dried)	15 mL
1 tsp	pepper	5 mL
1	clove garlic, minced	1
	Olive oil	

OLIVE PEPPER TAPENADE:

2	sweet red peppers	2
¼ cup	pitted oil-cured black olives	50 mL
1 tbsp	chopped fresh parsley	15 mL
1 tsp	Dijon mustard	5 mL
½ tsp	pepper	2 mL
1	clove garlic, minced	1
	Salt	

- Trim fat from lamb. Combine mustard, rosemary, pepper and garlic; rub all over lamb. Let stand for 1 hour at room temperature, or refrigerate for up to 8 hours.

- OLIVE PEPPER TAPENADE: Meanwhile, broil red peppers, turning often, for 15 to 20 minutes or until charred. Let cool; peel and seed, discarding stem and ribs. In food processor, chop red peppers, olives, parsley, mustard and pepper. Stir in garlic; season with salt to taste.

- Brush baking sheet lightly with oil; heat in 375°F (190°C) oven for 5 minutes. Place lamb on sheet; roast for 30 minutes or until meat thermometer registers 140°F (60°C) for rare.

- Transfer lamb to cutting board and tent with foil; let stand for 10 minutes. Spread with tapenade; carve into ¼-inch (5 mm) thick slices.

Makes 8 servings.
PER SERVING: about 220 calories, 30 g protein, 9 g fat, 3 g carbohydrate, good source iron.

Turkey Breast Spiral with Barley Timbales

Lean turkey breast stuffed and rolled makes a colorful year-round company dish.

1	pkg (10 oz/284 g) fresh spinach	1
2 tbsp	vegetable oil	25 mL
1	onion, chopped	1
3	cloves garlic, minced	3
1½ cups	ricotta cheese	375 mL
1	egg yolk	1
3 tbsp	freshly grated Parmesan cheese	50 mL
1 tsp	salt	5 mL
½ tsp	pepper	2 mL
¼ tsp	nutmeg	1 mL
1	boneless turkey breast (about 3 lb/1.5 kg)	1
½ cup	diced sweet red pepper	125 mL
¼ tsp	dried thyme	1 mL
2 tsp	all-purpose flour	10 mL
⅓ cup	chicken stock	75 mL
	Barley Timbales (recipe, page 127)	

- Trim and rinse spinach; shake off excess water. In saucepan, cook spinach, covered, with just the water clinging to leaves, over medium-high heat for about 5 minutes or just until wilted. Drain well and set aside.

- In small skillet, heat 2 tsp (10 mL) of the oil over medium heat; cook onion and garlic, stirring occasionally, for 3 minutes. Transfer to bowl; mix in ricotta, egg yolk, Parmesan cheese, half of the salt, half of the pepper, and the nutmeg.

- Butterfly turkey breast by slicing almost in half horizontally. Open up like book; cover with waxed paper and pound lightly until just under ½ inch (1 cm) thick. Spread with ricotta mixture; spread with spinach, then red pepper.

- Starting at narrow skinless end, roll up turkey so skin is on top and filling is enclosed. Tie at 3-inch (8 cm) intervals with kitchen string. Sprinkle with thyme and remaining salt and pepper.

- In roasting pan, heat remaining oil in 450°F (230°C) oven for 10 minutes. Reduce heat to 350°F (180°C); roast turkey roll, basting once, for 25 to 30 minutes or until juices run clear when turkey is pierced with fork. Transfer to platter and tent with foil; let stand for 10 minutes before slicing.

- Meanwhile, strain pan juices into small saucepan; whisk in flour. Whisk in stock; cook, whisking, over medium-high heat until boiling and slightly thickened. Spoon over turkey slices. Serve with Barley Timbales.

Makes 8 servings.
PER SERVING (without Timbales):
about 420 calories, 45 g protein, 23 g fat,
5 g carbohydrate, good source
calcium, excellent source iron.

Barley Timbales

A timbale is simply a mould to give this healthy grain and vegetable combo a more pleasing shape.

2½ cups	chicken stock	625 mL
1 cup	pearl or pot barley	250 mL
2 tbsp	butter	25 mL
½ tsp	each salt and pepper	2 mL
¼ tsp	dried thyme	1 mL
4	green onions, chopped	4
1 cup	diced carrots	250 mL
¼ cup	currants	50 mL

- In saucepan, bring stock, barley, butter, salt, pepper and thyme to boil; reduce heat, cover and simmer for 30 minutes.
- Stir in onions, carrots and currants; cook, covered, for 20 to 25 minutes or until liquid is absorbed and barley is tender. Pack into timbale moulds, small ramekins or ½-cup (125 mL) dry measures. Let stand for 3 minutes before inverting onto plates.

Makes 8 servings.

Per serving: about 150 calories, 4 g protein, 4 g fat, 26 g carbohydrate, high source fibre.

Wild Rice Pilaf

Here's how chef Bertha Skye dresses up wild rice, a crop grown in her native northern Saskatchewan.

1 cup	wild rice	250 mL
2 cups	parboiled rice	500 mL
2 tbsp	vegetable or olive oil	25 mL
1	clove garlic, minced	1
1	each sweet green and red pepper, diced	1
1½ cups	chopped celery	375 mL
6	green onions, chopped	6
6 cups	sliced mushrooms (1 lb/500 g)	1.5 L
¼ cup	soy sauce	50 mL
	Salt and pepper	

- In large saucepan, bring wild rice and 8 cups (2 L) water to boil; reduce heat and simmer for 25 minutes. Add white rice; simmer for 20 minutes or until tender; drain.
- Meanwhile, in wok or large skillet, heat oil over medium-high heat; stir-fry garlic, green and red peppers, celery, onions and mushrooms for about 10 minutes or until tender-crisp.
- Add rice; cook for 5 minutes or until heated through. Stir in soy sauce. Season with salt and pepper to taste.

Makes 8 servings.

Per serving: about 305 calories, 8 g protein, 4 g fat, 58 g carbohydrate, high source fibre.

Roast Potato Slices

Great with a roast, these potatoes with rosemary and olive oil are quite irresistible. Make more if you dare!

6	baking potatoes (about 3 lb/1.5 kg)	6
2 tbsp	chopped fresh rosemary (or 2 tsp/10 mL dried)	25 mL
2 tbsp	olive oil	25 mL
3	cloves garlic, minced	3
1½ tsp	salt	7 mL
¾ tsp	pepper	4 mL

- Scrub potatoes; cut into ¼-inch (5 mm) thick slices and place in bowl. Combine rosemary, oil, garlic, salt and pepper; toss with potatoes.
- Spread potatoes on nonstick or foil-lined baking sheet. Roast in 375°F (190°C) oven, stirring occasionally, for 40 to 45 minutes or until golden.

Makes 8 servings.

Per serving: about 155 calories, 3 g protein, 4 g fat, 29 g carbohydrate.

Osso Buco

*Here's delicious proof how good veal shanks are simmered
to melting tenderness with a tomato-based sauce.*

¼ cup	all-purpose flour	50 mL
	Salt and pepper	
4 lb	veal shanks, cut in 2-inch (5 cm) pieces	2 kg
¼ cup	olive oil	50 mL
4	stalks celery, chopped	4
3	carrots, chopped	3
2	onions, chopped	2
3	cloves garlic, minced	3
1½ cups	each white wine and chicken stock (or 3 cups/750 mL chicken stock)	375 mL
1 tsp	each dried sage and rosemary	5 mL
1	bay leaf	1
¼ cup	tomato paste	50 mL
GREMOLATA:		
½ cup	chopped fresh parsley	125 mL
2 tsp	grated lemon rind	10 mL
4	cloves garlic, minced	4

- In plastic bag, combine flour, 1 tsp (5 mL) salt and ½ tsp (2 mL) pepper; add veal, in batches, and shake to coat. In Dutch oven, heat oil over medium-high heat; brown veal, in batches. Remove and set aside.

- Add celery, carrots, onions and garlic to pan; cover and cook over low heat for about 8 minutes or until onions are softened.

- Return veal to pan. Stir in wine, chicken stock, sage, rosemary, ¼ tsp (1 mL) salt and bay leaf; bring to boil. Reduce heat, cover and simmer, stirring occasionally, for 60 to 70 minutes or until veal is tender.

- Stir tomato paste into pan; cook, uncovered, for about 15 minutes or until sauce is thickened. Season with salt and pepper to taste. Discard bay leaf.

- GREMOLATA: Meanwhile, in small bowl, combine parsley, lemon rind and garlic; sprinkle over each serving.

Makes 6 servings.
PER SERVING: about 490 calories, 50 g protein, 23 g fat, 17 g carbohydrate, excellent source iron.

Curried Mussels

Prince Edward Island's plump, clean, tasty mussels bring a touch of glamor and style to the table.

2 lb	mussels	1 kg
2 tbsp	vegetable oil	25 mL
1	onion, finely chopped	1
2	cloves garlic, minced	2
2 tsp	finely chopped gingerroot	10 mL
1 tbsp	curry powder	15 mL
½ cup	dry white wine or clam juice	125 mL
1 cup	whipping cream	250 mL
	Salt and pepper	
2 tbsp	chopped fresh coriander or green onion	25 mL

- In large heavy saucepan, heat oil over medium heat; cook onion, garlic and ginger, stirring, for 3 minutes. Add curry powder; cook, stirring, for 30 seconds. Add wine; bring to simmer over medium-high heat.

- Add mussels; cover and cook for 5 to 7 minutes or until mussels open, shaking pan occasionally. With slotted spoon, remove mussels and keep warm, discarding any that do not open.

- Bring liquid in pan to boil over high heat; boil for about 3 minutes or until reduced to ½ cup (125 mL). Pour in cream; boil for about 2 minutes or until thick enough to coat spoon. Season with salt and pepper to taste.

- Transfer mussels to serving dishes. Pour sauce over top; sprinkle with coriander. To eat, remove mussels from shells using fork, or empty hinged shells as pincers.

Makes 4 servings.
PER SERVING: about 340 calories, 10 g protein, 29 g fat, 8 g carbohydrate, good source iron.

- Scrub mussels under cold running water; remove any beards. Discard any mussels that do not close when tapped. Set aside.

Cioppino with Heart-Shaped Croutes

Mediterranean-inspired fish soups have always been favorites of our test kitchen and food writers. Here is the finest version, with touches of orange and fennel.

2 tsp	olive oil	10 mL
1	leek, thinly sliced	1
1	clove garlic, minced	1
1	strip orange rind	1
1	bay leaf	1
1 tbsp	tomato paste	15 mL
½ tsp	fennel seeds	2 mL
¼ tsp	dried thyme	1 mL
Pinch	each cayenne and saffron	Pinch
Pinch	each salt and pepper	Pinch
1	can (19 oz/540 mL) tomatoes, drained and diced	1
1½ cups	fish stock	375 mL
1 cup	clam juice	250 mL
½ cup	rotini pasta	125 mL
½ cup	white wine	125 mL
2	slices bread	2
¼ lb	white firm-fleshed fish	125 g
¼ lb	salmon	125 g
¼ lb	large raw shrimp	125 g
	Chopped fresh parsley	

- In large saucepan, heat oil over medium heat; cook leek and garlic, stirring, for 3 to 4 minutes or until softened.

- Add orange rind, bay leaf, tomato paste, fennel seeds, thyme, cayenne, saffron, salt and pepper; cook, stirring, for 1 minute.

- Add tomatoes, fish stock, clam juice, pasta and wine; bring to boil. Reduce heat and simmer for 15 to 20 minutes or until reduced slightly.

- Meanwhile, using heart-shaped cookie cutter, cut out hearts from each slice of bread; broil for about 2 minutes or until golden brown. Set aside.

- Remove skin from white fish and salmon; cut into 1½-inch (4 cm) chunks. Peel and devein shrimp. Add white fish and salmon to soup; cover and cook over medium-low heat for about 5 minutes or until almost opaque.

- Gently stir in shrimp; cover and cook for 5 to 7 minutes or until shrimp are pink. Discard orange rind and bay leaf. Serve garnished with croutes and parsley.

Makes 2 servings.

PER SERVING: about 405 calories, 38 g protein, 12 g fat, 33 g carbohydrate, high source fibre, excellent source iron.

TIP: Cut the bread for the "croutes" into shapes to suit the occasion; for example, hearts for Valentine's Day and people you love.

CHAPTER SEVEN

BREADS ON THE RISE

*Great moments in life
include baking your first loaf
of bread — whether you use
the tried-and-true way by
hand or go new-fangled with
a bread machine. Here's how
to discover what bread
makers have known for a
long time — bread is easy to
make and hardly anyone can
resist its fresh-baked aroma.*

Sesame Seed Bagels

These are Montreal-style bagels created in our test kitchen by ex-Montrealer and director Daphna Rabinovitch. And just what characterizes Montreal bagels? They're smaller, less puffed up than a lot of the buns masquerading as bagels and they taste good, even without smoked salmon and cream cheese.

1 tsp	granulated sugar	5 mL
1 cup	lukewarm water	250 mL
1	pkg active dry yeast (or 1 tbsp/15 mL)	1
2	eggs	2
1 tbsp	vegetable oil	15 mL
3½ cups	(approx) all-purpose flour	875 mL
2 tbsp	granulated sugar	25 mL
2 tsp	salt	10 mL
POACHING LIQUID:		
16 cups	water	4 L
2 tbsp	granulated sugar	25 mL
GLAZE:		
½ cup	sesame or poppy seeds	125 mL
1	egg, beaten	1

- In large bowl, dissolve 1 tsp (5 mL) sugar in water. Sprinkle in yeast; let stand for 10 minutes or until frothy. Whisk in eggs and oil. Beat in 2 cups (500 mL) of the flour, sugar and salt until smooth. Gradually stir in enough of the remaining flour to make soft but not sticky dough.

> **TIPS**
> - Be sure to press the ends of the dough together very firmly, otherwise the bagels will come apart in the water.
> - The bagels can be wrapped well and frozen for up to two weeks.

- Turn out onto lightly floured surface; knead for 8 to 10 minutes or until smooth and elastic. Place in greased bowl, turning to grease all over. Cover with plastic wrap; let rise in warm place for 1 to 1½ hours or until doubled in bulk.

- Punch down dough; knead several times. Divide into 12 equal portions; roll each into 12-inch (30 cm) rope, covering pieces with tea towel as you work. Bring ends of dough together, overlapping by about 1 inch (2.5 cm) and stretching overlap around other end to meet underneath; pinch firmly to seal. Place on floured baking sheet; cover with tea towel and let rise for 15 minutes.

- POACHING LIQUID: In wide saucepan, bring water to boil; add sugar. Slip bagels into water, 3 or 4 at a time; cook over medium heat for 1 minute. Turn; cook for 1 minute. Using slotted spatula, remove bagels to well-greased or parchment paper-lined baking sheets.

- GLAZE: Place sesame seeds in dish. Brush egg over bagels. Dip egg side of bagels into seeds; return to baking sheet. Bake in 400°F (200°C) oven for 20 to 25 minutes or until tops are golden and bottoms sound hollow when tapped. Let cool on racks.

Makes 12 bagels.
PER BAGEL: about 210 calories, 7 g protein, 6 g fat, 32 g carbohydrate, good source iron.

VARIATION
WHOLE WHEAT CINNAMON RAISIN BAGELS: Substitute 1 cup (250 mL) whole wheat flour for 1 cup (250 mL) all-purpose flour. Increase 2 tbsp (25 mL) sugar to ¼ cup (50 mL). Stir in 2 tsp (10 mL) cinnamon along with eggs. After punching down dough, thoroughly knead in 1 cup (250 mL) raisins. Omit sesame seeds.

Bagels are beautiful, especially when captured in full color by Canadian Living's original food photographer, Fred Bird.

Hot Cross Buns

Hot cross buns were once available only on Good Friday. But their spicy flavor and moist fruitiness were just too good to restrict to one day and the glazed buns are now often available throughout the winter.

¼ cup	lukewarm water	50 mL
½ cup	granulated sugar	125 mL
1	pkg active dry yeast (or 1 tbsp/15 mL)	1
3½ cups	all-purpose flour	875 mL
2 tbsp	cinnamon	25 mL
1 tsp	nutmeg	5 mL
½ tsp	salt	2 mL
¼ tsp	ground cloves	1 mL
¾ cup	warm milk	175 mL
¼ cup	butter, melted	50 mL
1	egg	1
1	egg yolk	1
½ cup	currants	125 mL
¼ cup	chopped mixed candied peel	50 mL
GLAZE:		
2 tbsp	each granulated sugar and water	25 mL
ICING:		
½ cup	icing sugar	125 mL
2 tsp	water	10 mL

- In small bowl, combine warm water with 1 tbsp (15 mL) of the sugar. Sprinkle in yeast; let stand for 10 minutes or until frothy.

- Meanwhile, in large bowl, blend together remaining sugar, flour, cinnamon, nutmeg, salt and cloves; make well in centre. Whisk together milk, butter, egg and egg yolk; pour into well. Pour in yeast mixture. With wooden spoon, stir until soft dough forms.

- Turn out onto lightly floured surface; knead for about 8 minutes or until smooth and elastic. Place in lightly greased bowl, turning to grease all over. Cover with plastic wrap; let rise in warm place for about 1 hour or until doubled in bulk.

- Punch down dough and turn out onto floured surface; knead in currants and peel. Shape into 12-inch (30 cm) log; cut into 9 even pieces. Stretch, tuck and pinch sides of dough all around to meet underneath to form balls.

- Place 2 inches (5 cm) apart on greased baking sheet. Cover lightly with tea towel; let rise for 35 minutes or until impression remains when dough is poked. Bake in 400°F (200°C) oven for about 16 minutes or until golden brown.

- GLAZE: In saucepan, stir sugar with water over medium heat until dissolved. Brush over buns. Let cool.

- ICING: Stir together icing sugar and water. Using piping bag fitted with round tip, pipe cross on top of each cooled bun.

Makes 9 buns.

PER BUN: about 355 calories, 7 g protein, 7 g fat, 65 g carbohydrate, good source iron.

VARIATION

BREAD MACHINE HOT CROSS LOAF: Reduce flour to 3¼ cups (800 mL). To baking pan from 2 lb (1 kg) bread machine, add (in order) water, milk, butter, sugar, eggs, salt, flour, cinnamon, nutmeg, cloves and yeast. Choose "sweet dough" setting; after first kneading (see machine instructions for time), add currants and peel.

TIP: To make 18 buns by hand, increase the yeast to 4 tsp (20 mL) and double the other ingredients.

Deep-Dish Pizza Bread

This deep-dish quick bread with pizza flavors is perfect for potlucks and picnics.

1½ cups	all-purpose flour	375 mL
⅓ cup	freshly grated Parmesan cheese	75 mL
½ cup	chopped sweet red pepper	125 mL
⅓ cup	chopped green onion	75 mL
2½ tsp	baking powder	12 mL
2 tsp	dried oregano	10 mL
1 tsp	granulated sugar	5 mL
½ tsp	each salt and pepper	2 mL
1 cup	milk	250 mL
⅓ cup	vegetable oil	75 mL
1	egg	1
12	thin slices pepperoni	12
¼ cup	shredded part-skim mozzarella cheese	50 mL

- In large bowl, stir together flour, Parmesan cheese, ⅓ cup (75 mL) of the red pepper, green onion, baking powder, oregano, sugar, salt and pepper. Whisk together milk, oil and egg. Pour over dry ingredients; stir just until moistened.

- Pour batter into lightly greased 8-inch (1.2 L) round cake pan. Arrange pepperoni over top; sprinkle with remaining red pepper and mozzarella cheese.

- Bake in 350°F (180°C) oven for about 35 minutes or until tester inserted in centre comes out clean. Let cool in pan.

Makes 6 servings.
PER SERVING: about 325 calories, 10 g protein, 19 g fat, 29 g carbohydrate, good source calcium.

Orange Poppy Seed Rolls

Barbara and Wendy's Country Bakery in Ancaster, Ontario, makes these hearty rolls. For loaves, let rise in two loaf pans and bake in 375°F (190°C) oven for 45 minutes.

2½ cups	lukewarm water	625 mL
1	pkg active dry yeast (or 1 tbsp/15 mL)	1
5 cups	(approx) all-purpose flour	1.25 L
⅓ cup	liquid honey	75 mL
1	seedless orange	1
¼ cup	rolled oats	50 mL
3 tbsp	poppy seeds	50 mL
2 tbsp	vegetable oil	25 mL
1 tsp	salt	5 mL
3½ cups	whole wheat flour	875 mL
½ cup	chopped dates	125 mL
	Melted butter	

- In large bowl, whisk together water, yeast, 2 cups (500 mL) of the all-purpose flour and honey until smooth. Cover and let stand in warm place for about 30 minutes or until foamy.

- Quarter orange; chop finely in food processor. Stir into yeast mixture along with oats, poppy seeds, oil and salt. Toss whole wheat flour with dates; stir into yeast mixture. Stir in enough of the remaining all-purpose flour to make firm, slightly sticky dough.

- Turn out dough onto lightly floured surface; knead, adding all-purpose flour as needed, for 10 to 12 minutes or until smooth and elastic. Place in greased bowl, turning to grease all over. Cover with plastic wrap; let rise for about 1 hour or until doubled in bulk.

- Punch down dough; turn out onto lightly floured surface and knead for 2 minutes. Let rest for 2 minutes. Shape into 24 rolls. Place on greased baking sheets. Cover and let rise for 30 to 45 minutes or until impression remains when dough is poked.

- Bake in 400°F (200°C) oven for 20 to 25 minutes or until golden brown and rolls sound hollow when tapped on bottom. Let cool on racks. Brush with butter.

Makes 24 rolls.
PER ROLL: about 195 calories, 6 g protein, 2 g fat, 39 g carbohydrate, high source fibre.

Rosemary Focaccia

A best-seller from Lesley Stowe Fine Foods in Vancouver, this golden round topped with onions and rosemary is a fine starter to dinner.

¼ cup	(approx) olive oil	50 mL
1	onion, chopped	1
½ tsp	granulated sugar	2 mL
1½ cups	lukewarm water	375 mL
1½ tsp	active dry yeast	7 mL
2 tbsp	olive oil	25 mL
½ tsp	salt	2 mL
3 cups	(approx) all-purpose flour	750 mL
4 tsp	chopped fresh rosemary	20 mL
	Cornmeal and coarse salt	

- In skillet, heat ¼ cup (50 mL) oil over low heat; cook onion, stirring occasionally, for 30 minutes or until golden. Let cool. Meanwhile, in large bowl, dissolve sugar in water. Sprinkle in yeast; let stand for 10 minutes or until frothy. Stir in 2 tbsp (25 mL) oil and salt. Add 2 cups (500 mL) of the flour and beat with electric mixer for 2 minutes or until smooth and elastic. With wooden spoon, gradually stir in remaining flour, onions and 1 tbsp (15 mL) of the rosemary.

- Turn out onto floured surface; knead, adding flour as needed, until smooth and elastic. Place in greased bowl, turning to grease all over. Cover with plastic wrap; let rise for 35 to 45 minutes or until doubled in bulk.

- Punch down dough; divide in half and pat each into flat round. Let rest for 5 minutes; stretch into 10-inch (25 cm) rounds. Place on greased baking sheets sprinkled with cornmeal. Cover and let rise for 35 to 45 minutes or until doubled in height. Brush with more oil; sprinkle with coarse salt and remaining rosemary. Bake in 375°F (190°C) oven for 25 to 30 minutes or until bottom is browned and crisp. Let cool on racks for 10 minutes. Cut into wedges to serve.

Makes 2 rounds, 12 wedges each.
PER WEDGE: about 90 calories, 2 g protein, 4 g fat, 13 g carbohydrate.

Clockwise from top: Pain de campagne, Black Bean Raisin Bread, Orange and Poppy Seed Bread, Gunn's Cheese Onion Buns, Rosemary Focaccia and Orange Poppy Seed Rolls

Pain de campagne

At the Boulangerie au Pain Doré in Montreal, this round cracked-wheat country loaf is a popular choice.

1 cup	coarse cracked wheat	250 mL
6 cups	(approx) all-purpose flour	1.5 L
1	pkg quick-rising yeast (or 1 tbsp/15 mL)	1
1 tbsp	granulated sugar	15 mL
2 tsp	salt	10 mL
2 cups	lukewarm water	500 mL

- In large bowl, pour 3 cups (750 mL) boiling water over cracked wheat. Let stand for 30 minutes; drain.

- Meanwhile, in large bowl, combine half of the flour, the yeast, sugar and salt; add lukewarm water and beat with electric mixer for about 3 minutes or until smooth and elastic. Cover with plastic wrap; let rise for 30 to 40 minutes or until bubbly and light. Stir down. With wooden spoon, stir in cracked wheat and enough of the remaining flour to make soft dough.

- Turn out onto lightly floured surface; knead for 8 to 10 minutes or until smooth and elastic. Place in greased bowl, turning to grease all over. Cover and let rise for 45 to 60 minutes or until doubled in bulk.

- Punch down dough; turn out onto lightly floured surface and divide in half. Knead each into smooth ball, stretching dough down all around and tucking underneath to shape. Let rest for 2 minutes; repeat stretching and tucking to tighten shape. Place on large greased baking sheet. Cover and let rise for 45 minutes.

- Slash top of each loaf; bake in 450°F (230°C) oven for 20 minutes. Reduce temperature to 375°F (190°C); bake for 20 to 30 minutes or until loaves sound hollow when tapped on bottom. Let cool on racks.

Makes 2 loaves, 12 slices each.
Per slice: about 137 calories, 4 g protein, trace fat, 29 g carbohydrate.

Black Bean Raisin Bread

From LaHave Bakery in Lunenburg County, Nova Scotia, comes Gael Watson's terrific variation of raisin bread.

1½ cups	dried black beans	375 mL
1 cup	raisins	250 mL
1 tsp	granulated sugar	5 mL
¼ cup	lukewarm water	50 mL
1	pkg active dry yeast (or 1 tbsp/15 mL)	1
¼ cup	fancy molasses	50 mL
2 tbsp	vegetable oil	25 mL
2 tsp	salt	10 mL
3 cups	whole wheat flour	750 mL
4 cups	(approx) all-purpose flour	1 L
1	egg	1

- In saucepan, bring beans and 8 cups (2 L) water to boil. Reduce heat, cover and simmer for 1 hour or until tender. Drain, reserving 2 cups (500 mL) of the cooking water; purée beans.

- In bowl, combine raisins with ½ cup (125 mL) of the hot bean water; set aside.

- In separate bowl, dissolve sugar in lukewarm water. Sprinkle in yeast; let stand for 10 minutes or until frothy.

- In large bowl, whisk together molasses, oil, raisins and bean water, salt and yeast mixture. Using electric mixer, beat in whole wheat flour; beat for 2 minutes. With wooden spoon, gradually stir in enough of the all-purpose flour to make firm, slightly sticky dough.

- Turn out onto lightly floured surface; knead, adding flour as needed, for 10 to 12 minutes or until smooth and elastic. Place in greased bowl, turning to grease all over. Cover with plastic wrap; let rise for 1½ to 2 hours or until doubled in bulk.

- Punch down dough; cut into thirds. Shape into round loaves. Place on greased baking sheets; cover and let rise for 45 minutes or until doubled. Beat egg with 1 tbsp (15 mL) water; brush over loaves. Bake in 375°F (190°C) oven for 45 to 50 minutes or until loaves sound hollow when tapped on bottom. Let cool on racks.

Makes 3 loaves, 10 slices each.
Per slice: about 170 calories, 6 g protein, 2 g fat, 34 g carbohydrate, high source fibre.

Gunn's Cheese Onion Buns

It's a rare customer who goes into Gunn's, one of Winnipeg's most durable Jewish bakeries, and doesn't come out with more items than were on the shopping list — such as these scrumptious melt-in-the-mouth buns.

2 cups	warm milk	500 mL
2 tbsp	granulated sugar	25 mL
1	pkg active dry yeast (or 1 tbsp/15 mL)	1
⅓ cup	granulated sugar	75 mL
2	eggs	2
⅓ cup	vegetable oil	75 mL
2 tsp	salt	10 mL
6½ cups	(approx) all-purpose flour	1.625 L

FILLING AND GLAZE:

2 tbsp	butter, melted	25 mL
3 cups	shredded old Cheddar cheese	750 mL
¼ cup	poppy seeds	50 mL
1	egg, lightly beaten	1
2	onions, sliced	2
½ cup	mayonnaise	125 mL

- In small bowl, combine milk with 2 tbsp (25 mL) sugar. Sprinkle in yeast; let stand for 10 minutes or until frothy.

- Meanwhile, in large bowl and using electric mixer, beat ⅓ cup (75 mL) sugar with eggs for 7 minutes or until thick and pale yellow. Stir in yeast mixture along with oil and salt. Beat in 4 cups (1 L) of the flour; with wooden spoon, stir in enough of the remaining flour to make firm, slightly sticky dough.

- Turn out onto lightly floured surface; knead, adding flour as needed, for 10 to 12 minutes or until smooth and elastic. Place in greased bowl, turning to grease all over. Cover with plastic wrap; let rise for 2 hours or until doubled. Punch down dough; divide in half. Roll out each half into 16- x 12-inch (40 x 30 cm) rectangle.

- FILLING AND GLAZE: Brush each rectangle with butter, leaving ½-inch (1 cm) border uncovered; sprinkle each with Cheddar cheese and poppy seeds. Brush egg over long edges. Starting at long side, roll up tightly; pinch seam to seal. Cut into ¾-inch (2 cm) thick slices; place on greased baking sheet. Cover and let rise for 1½ to 2 hours or until impression remains when dough is poked.

- Brush buns with egg. Sprinkle with onions. Top each with 1 tsp (5 mL) mayonnaise. Bake in 375°F (190°C) oven for 25 to 30 minutes or until golden and buns sound hollow when tapped on bottom. Let cool on racks.

Makes 20 buns.

PER BUN: about 355 calories, 11 g protein, 17 g fat, 39 g carbohydrate, good source calcium and iron.

FLOUR POWER

Canada produces the finest wheat in the world, with a high protein content. (In fact, Italy imports Canadian durum wheat to make pasta.)

- All-purpose flour is a mixture of 80 per cent hard wheat and 20 per cent soft wheat. Because our wheat has such a high protein content, Canadians can use all-purpose flour for their loaves of bread and still get fabulous results.

- Whole wheat flour is milled from the entire wheat kernel, including the bran and germ. Whole wheat flour has a strong flavor and high nutritional value.

- New bread flours are appearing on the market in response to the popularity of the bread machine. Because gluten flour has been added to flours for the bread machine, the loaves have an increased amount of protein and produce bread with higher volume and softer, more even texture.

- Store all flours in airtight containers and store whole wheat flour in the refrigerator or freezer to prevent it from going rancid.

Homemade Pizza Base

Here's how to make two baked pizza bases that can be frozen to top later with your favorite toppings, or dressed and baked immediately.

1 tsp	granulated sugar	10 mL
1 cup	lukewarm water	250 mL
1	pkg active dry yeast (or 1 tbsp/15 mL)	1
2¼ cups	(approx) all-purpose flour	550 mL
¼ cup	cornmeal or rye flour	50 mL
1 tbsp	olive oil	15 mL
1 tsp	salt	5 mL

- In large bowl, dissolve sugar in water. Sprinkle in yeast; stir to dissolve. Let stand for 10 minutes or until frothy.

- With electric mixer, gradually beat in 1 cup (250 mL) of the flour, cornmeal, oil and salt; beat for about 3 minutes or until smooth. Mix in enough of the remaining flour to make moderately stiff dough.

TIP: If you prefer to make pizza right away, add toppings of your choice to unbaked base; bake in 500°F (260°C) oven for about 12 minutes or until crust is golden and topping bubbling.

- Turn out dough onto lightly floured surface; knead for 10 minutes or until smooth and elastic, adding more flour if very sticky. Shape into ball. Place in greased bowl, turning to grease all over. Cover and let rise in warm place for 1 to 1½ hours or until doubled in bulk.

- Punch down dough and halve; roll out each portion into 13-inch (33 cm) circle. Transfer to 12-inch (30 cm) cornmeal-dusted pizza pan; fold edges under to make raised border.

- Cover base with waxed paper; weigh down with pie weights. Bake in 450°F (230°C) oven for 10 minutes or until lightly browned. Let cool. (*Pizza bases can be wrapped in plastic wrap, overwrapped in foil and frozen for up to 2 weeks.*)

Makes 2 pizza bases, enough for 4 servings.
PER BASE: about 665 calories, 17 g protein, 9 g fat, 126 g carbohydrate, very high source fibre, excellent source iron.

Jalapeño Corn Quick Bread

Making bread with yeast doesn't take a lot of time, but it does take planning. For those occasions when you want a personalized bread and the clock has ticked past yeast-rising time, make a quick bread — this luxurious cornbread, for example.

1¼ cups	cornmeal	300 mL
1 cup	shredded old Cheddar cheese	250 mL
¾ cup	all-purpose flour	175 mL
½ tsp	each salt and baking soda	2 mL
3	eggs, beaten	3
1	can (10 oz/284 mL) creamed corn	1
¾ cup	buttermilk	175 mL
⅓ cup	vegetable oil	75 mL
2 tbsp	chopped pickled jalapeño pepper	25 mL

- In large bowl, stir together cornmeal, cheese, flour, salt and baking soda.

- Whisk together eggs, corn, buttermilk, oil and jalapeño pepper; stir into cornmeal mixture just until combined.

- Pour into greased 8-inch (2 L) square cake pan, smoothing top; bake in 400°F (200°C) oven for 35 to 40 minutes or until golden and tester inserted in centre comes out clean.

Makes 8 servings.
PER SERVING: about 325 calories, 10 g protein, 16 g fat, 34 g carbohydrate.

Beth Moffatt's Armenian Flatbread

Crisp flatbread, more like a mega-cracker than a loaf of bread, is very popular. Using former test kitchen manager Beth Moffatt's recipe, you can make this impressive bread at home.

½ cup	warm water	125 mL
4	egg whites	4
1 tbsp	butter, melted	15 mL
1 tsp	salt	5 mL
1 tsp	granulated sugar	5 mL
1 tsp	active dry yeast	5 mL
2½ cups	(approx) all-purpose flour	625 mL
1 tbsp	each sesame and poppy seeds	15 mL

- In bowl, combine water, egg whites, butter, salt, sugar and yeast. Using wooden spoon, stir in 2 cups (500 mL) of the flour; beat until smooth. Add enough of the remaining flour to form soft dough.

- Turn out dough onto lightly floured surface; knead several times or until dough holds together. Place in greased bowl, turning to grease all over. Cover with plastic wrap; let rise in warm place for about 1¼ hours or until doubled in bulk.

- Punch down dough and turn out onto lightly floured surface; divide into 4 portions. Roll out each portion into ⅛-inch (3 mm) thick circle. Place on lightly greased baking sheets. Prick all over with fork. Brush lightly with water; sprinkle with sesame seeds and poppy seeds.

- Bake in 400°F (200°C) oven for about 15 minutes or until golden brown. Remove from baking sheets and let cool on racks. Cut each into 8 wedges.

Makes 32 pieces.
PER PIECE: about 45 calories, 2 g protein, 1 g fat, 8 g carbohydrate.

Country Seed Bread

*You can found your reputation as a bread maker on this healthy loaf — as good kneaded by hand
as it is worked into a tall loaf in the machine. It makes great toast and unbeatable sandwiches.*

1 ¼ cups	water	300 mL
2 tbsp	liquid honey	25 mL
2 tbsp	vegetable oil	25 mL
1 ½ tsp	salt	7 mL
2 cups	(approx) all-purpose flour	500 mL
1 cup	whole wheat flour	250 mL
¼ cup	flax seeds	50 mL
2 tbsp	sesame seeds	25 mL
1 tbsp	poppy seeds	15 mL
2 tsp	quick-rising dry yeast	10 mL

HAND METHOD

- In small bowl, whisk together water, honey, oil and salt. In large bowl, stir together all-purpose and whole wheat flours, flax, sesame and poppy seeds and yeast. Stir honey mixture into flour mixture until sticky dough forms.

- Turn out onto lightly floured surface; knead for about 8 minutes or until elastic yet still slightly sticky, adding up to ¼ cup (50 mL) more all-purpose flour if necessary. Place in lightly greased bowl, turning to grease all over. Cover with plastic wrap; let rise in warm place for about 1 ¼ hours or until doubled in bulk.

- Punch down dough and turn out onto lightly floured surface; gently pull into 11- x 8-inch (28 x 20 cm) rectangle. Starting at narrow end, roll up into cylinder; press down at seam to seal. Place, seam side down, in greased 8- x 4-inch (1.5 L) loaf pan. Cover with tea towel; let rise in warm place for 1 hour or until doubled in bulk and risen ¾ inch (2 cm) above rim of pan.

- Brush top of loaf with water. Using serrated knife, make one 1-inch (2.5 cm) deep cut lengthwise through top of loaf. Bake in 400°F (200°C) oven for 15 minutes; reduce heat to 350°F (180°C); bake for 30 to 35 minutes or until top is browned and bottom sounds hollow when tapped. Remove from pan; let cool completely on rack.

Makes 1 loaf, 12 slices.

LARGE BREAD MACHINE

- Remove baking pan from large (1 ½ to 2 lb/750 g to 1 kg) bread machine. Add to pan (in order) water, honey, oil, salt, all-purpose and whole wheat flours, flax seeds, sesame seeds and poppy seeds. Sprinkle yeast over top, making sure yeast does not touch water mixture.

- According to manufacturer's instructions, choose cycle appropriate to nonsweet- or nonfresh-milk bread. When baked, immediately remove pan from machine; shake loaf from pan. Let cool completely on rack.

Makes 1 loaf, 12 slices.
PER SLICE: about 175 calories, 5 g protein, 5 g fat, 28 g carbohydrate.

VARIATION

SMALL BREAD MACHINE

¾ cup	water	175 mL
4 tsp	liquid honey	20 mL
4 tsp	vegetable oil	20 mL
1 tsp	salt	5 mL
1 ⅓ cups	all-purpose flour	325 mL
⅔ cup	whole wheat flour	150 mL
3 tbsp	flax seeds	50 mL
4 tsp	sesame seeds	20 mL
2 tsp	poppy seeds	10 mL
1 ¼ tsp	quick-rising dry yeast	6 mL

- Remove baking pan from small (1 lb/500 g) bread machine; follow method for large bread machine but with these reduced amounts.

Makes 1 loaf, 8 slices.

TIP: For a nuttier flavor, toast flax, sesame and poppy seeds in skillet over medium heat for 4 minutes, stirring often; let cool completely.

Bread Machine Potato Bread

For generations, bakers have added mashed potatoes and the cooking water to bread, giving it a pleasant moistness and even texture. When you cook potatoes for the evening meal, cook extra for bread.

1	small potato, peeled and halved	1
3 tbsp	vegetable oil	50 mL
2 tbsp	granulated sugar	25 mL
1½ tsp	salt	7 mL
3 cups	all-purpose flour	750 mL
1½ tsp	quick-rising dry yeast (or 1¼ tsp/6 mL bread machine yeast)	7 mL

- In saucepan of boiling salted water, cook potato for 10 to 15 minutes or until tender; drain, reserving ¾ cup (175 mL) cooking water. Mash potato well to make ½ cup (125 mL). Let potato and cooking liquid cool to room temperature.

- Remove baking pan from large (1½ to 2 lb/750 g to 1 kg) bread machine. Add to pan (in order) cooking water, oil, sugar, salt, mashed potato and flour. Sprinkle yeast over top, making sure yeast does not touch water mixture.

- According to manufacturer's instructions, choose cycle appropriate to nonsweet- or nonfresh-milk bread. When baked, immediately remove pan from machine; shake loaf from pan. Let cool completely on rack.

Makes 1 loaf, 12 slices.
PER SLICE: about 160 calories, 4 g protein, 4 g fat, 28 g carbohydrate.

BREAD MACHINE TIPS

- Read your manual! Every bread machine is different.
- Be sure you are using the setting or cycle on your machine that is correct for the type of bread you are baking.
- Add the ingredients to the pan in the order listed.
- Place machine well away from counter edge. Occasionally, a machine will move during the knead cycle.
- Do not open lid of machine once the proof cycle begins. If you must peek, do so while machine is kneading dough.

- If a baked loaf sticks to the pan, rap a top corner of the pan against the countertop to help shake bread loose, or use a plastic spatula to ease out loaf. Don't use a knife or metal spatula; you may damage the nonstick coating.
- If the blade is stuck in the loaf, use a small knife to pry it loose. If blade sticks to pan, soak in warm water for 15 minutes, then remove.
- If the crust is too dark, use the setting for sweet bread on your machine.

Crusty Bread with Cornmeal

If you set your bread-machine timer, you can wake up to thick slices of this golden-hued bread.

1⅓ cups	water	325 mL
¼ tsp	hot pepper sauce	1 mL
3 tbsp	vegetable oil	50 mL
1 tbsp	granulated sugar	15 mL
1½ tsp	salt	7 mL
¾ cup	cornmeal	175 mL
3¼ cups	all-purpose flour	800 mL
1½ tsp	quick-rising dry yeast (or 1¼ tsp/6 mL bread machine yeast)	7 mL

- Remove baking pan from large (1½ to 2 lb/750 g to 1 kg) bread machine. Add to pan (in order) water, hot pepper sauce, oil, sugar, salt, cornmeal and flour. Sprinkle yeast over top, making sure yeast does not touch water mixture.

- According to manufacturer's instructions, choose cycle appropriate to nonsweet- or nonfresh-milk bread. When baked, immediately remove pan from machine; shake loaf from pan. Let cool completely on rack.

Makes 1 loaf, 12 slices.
PER SLICE: about 190 calories, 4 g protein, 4 g fat, 33 g carbohydrate.

Cinnamon Braided Egg Bread

Cinnamon-rich and currant-studded, this easy-to-make bread is a wonderful way to welcome brunch guests. The technique of mixing the yeast into the flour is a foolproof one that makes even beginner yeast bakers look like experts.

2	pkg active dry yeast (or 2 tbsp/25 mL)	2
⅓ cup	granulated sugar	75 mL
2 tsp	salt	10 mL
6 cups	(approx) all-purpose flour	1.5 L
1¾ cups	water	425 mL
4	eggs, lightly beaten	4
½ cup	butter, melted	125 mL
1 cup	currants	250 mL
¼ cup	dark rum or water	50 mL
¼ cup	cinnamon	50 mL
1 tbsp	light cream or milk	15 mL
GLAZE:		
1 cup	icing sugar	250 mL
2 tbsp	lemon juice	25 mL

- In large bowl, whisk together yeast, sugar, salt and 2 cups (500 mL) of the flour. Heat water until hot yet bearable to the touch, 120°F (50°C); whisk into flour mixture along with eggs and butter until smooth. With wooden spoon, stir in enough of the remaining flour, ½ cup (125 mL) at a time, to make dough that is too stiff to stir.

- Turn out onto lightly floured surface; knead for about 10 minutes or until smooth and elastic, adding flour as necessary. Meanwhile, gently heat currants with rum until liquid is absorbed; let cool slightly. Knead currants into dough. Place in greased bowl, turning to grease all over. Cover with plastic wrap; let rise in warm place for about 1 hour or until doubled in bulk.

- Sprinkle cinnamon on large tray. Punch down dough and turn out onto floured surface; divide into 6 pieces. Roll each piece into 18-inch (46 cm) strip; roll in cinnamon. Lay 3 strips side by side. Braid each set of strips from middle to each end; tuck ends under. Place loaves in 2 greased 9- x 5-inch (2 L) loaf pans; cover loosely with plastic wrap. Let rise until almost doubled in bulk, about 30 minutes.

- Brush loaves with cream. Bake in 350°F (180°C) oven for 35 to 40 minutes or until loaves sound hollow when tapped on bottom. Let cool completely on racks.

- GLAZE: Whisk sugar with lemon juice until smooth; drizzle over loaves.

Makes 2 loaves, 16 slices each.
PER SLICE: about 160 calories, 4 g protein, 4 g fat, 28 g carbohydrate.

CHAPTER EIGHT

BRIGHT BEGINNINGS

It takes more than a coffee to start the day. Nutritionists have joined Mom in extolling the benefits of a good breakfast. It will make us smarter and put us in a better mood. Here are some fresh ideas for weekday starters and treats for the weekend.

Chocolate Buttermilk Waffles with Strawberries

Pretty decadent, what with chocolate and all! But enjoy the fact that the waffles are made with low-fat cocoa and buttermilk and topped with vitamin C–rich strawberries.

1 cup	all-purpose flour	250 mL
⅔ cup	granulated sugar	150 mL
½ cup	sifted unsweetened cocoa powder	125 mL
¾ tsp	cinnamon	4 mL
½ tsp	baking powder	2 mL
½ tsp	baking soda	2 mL
1 cup	buttermilk	250 mL
2	eggs, separated	2
¼ cup	butter, melted	50 mL
½ tsp	vanilla	2 mL
	Butter	
TOPPING:		
3 cups	sliced strawberries	750 mL
1½ tsp	granulated sugar	7 mL

- TOPPING: In small bowl, toss strawberries with sugar; set aside.

- In large bowl, stir together flour, sugar, cocoa, cinnamon, baking powder and baking soda; make well in centre. Pour in buttermilk, egg yolks, butter and vanilla; whisk into flour mixture.

- In separate bowl, beat egg whites until soft peaks form; fold one-quarter into batter. Fold in remaining whites.

- For waffles, heat waffle machine and cook according to manufacturer's directions, using ⅓ cup (75 mL) batter for each waffle.

- For pancakes, heat griddle or large nonstick skillet over medium heat; brush with butter. Using ¼ cup (50 mL) batter for each pancake and brushing pan with more butter as necessary, cook for about 2½ minutes or until bubbles break on top but do not fill in. Turn and cook for 2 minutes. Serve topped with strawberries.

Makes 10 waffles or 12 pancakes.
PER WAFFLE: about 195 calories, 4 g protein, 7 g fat, 30 g carbohydrate.

Paw-Print Pancakes

Whether they're Bigfoot or domestic doggie-size, these "cakes" are a hit. Make them with the Pancake Quick Mix and serve with Baked Sausage Patties and Apple Compote Topping (see photo above).

2	eggs	2
2 cups	apple juice or water	500 mL
1 cup	mashed banana or applesauce	250 mL
4 cups	Pancake Quick Mix (recipe, page 149)	1 L

TIP: For hearts, letters and numbers, funnel batter into a squeeze bottle and "write" in the skillet.

- In bowl, stir together eggs, apple juice and banana; stir in pancake mix.

- Heat greased nonstick skillet over medium heat. Using ¼ cup (50 mL) batter for each pancake, pour one-third into pan in oval shape; spoon in remaining batter in 4 drops, attaching to oval to form shape of paw.

- Cook for 2 minutes or until bottom is golden and bubbles break on top but do not fill in; turn and cook until bottom is golden.

Makes 24 pancakes.
PER SERVING OF 3 PANCAKES: about 315 calories, 7 g protein, 13 g fat, 42 g carbohydrate.

Pancake Quick Mix

Have your own pancake mix on hand. It's inexpensive and so easy to use.

5 cups	all-purpose flour	1.25 L
2 cups	instant skim milk powder	500 mL
3 tbsp	granulated sugar	50 mL
3 tbsp	baking powder	50 mL
2 tbsp	cinnamon	25 mL
2 tsp	baking soda	10 mL
1 tsp	salt	5 mL
1¼ cups	shortening	300 mL

- In bowl, combine flour, milk powder, sugar, baking powder, cinnamon, baking soda and salt.
- Using pastry blender or 2 knives, cut in shortening until mixture is in coarse crumbs. *(Mix can be refrigerated in airtight container for up to 2 months.)*

Makes about 11 cups (2.75 L).

Baked Sausage Patties

Extra herbs jazz up bulk sausage meat. You can form and refrigerate patties the day before serving.

1 lb	sausage meat	500 g
½ cup	dry bread crumbs	125 mL
3	green onions, finely chopped	3
2 tbsp	chopped fresh parsley	25 mL
½ tsp	dried thyme	2 mL
¼ tsp	pepper	1 mL

- In bowl, combine sausage, ¼ cup (50 mL) of the crumbs, onions, parsley, thyme and pepper. Shape into eight ¼-inch (5 mm) thick patties.
- Lightly coat patties with remaining crumbs. Bake on rack in roasting pan in 375°F (190°C) oven for 20 minutes or until no longer pink inside, turning once.

Makes 8 servings.
Per serving: about 225 calories, 9 g protein, 18 g fat, 6 g carbohydrate.

Apple Compote Topping

Fruit and fruit syrups are fresh alternatives for topping pancakes and waffles.

6	large apples	6
¼ cup	lemon juice	50 mL
⅓ cup	packed brown sugar	75 mL
1 tsp	cinnamon	5 mL
¼ tsp	nutmeg	1 mL
2 tbsp	butter (optional)	25 mL
¼ cup	toasted almonds, chopped	50 mL

- Peel and core apples; cut into thick slices. Place in baking dish; toss with lemon juice. Combine sugar, cinnamon and nutmeg; mix lightly with apples. Dot with butter (if using).
- Cover and bake in 400°F (200°C) oven for 15 minutes; stir. Bake for 25 minutes longer or until tender. Garnish with almonds.

Makes 8 servings.
Per serving: about 140 calories, 1 g protein, 2 g fat, 32 g carbohydrate.

> Tip: To toast almonds, pecans or walnuts, bake on baking sheet in 350°F (180°C) oven for 5 to 10 minutes or until fragrant. Or microwave at High for 6 to 8 minutes, rearranging occasionally.

Sweet Potato Waffles

Waffles or pancakes — it's your choice. The sweet potato, one of nature's densest nutrient packages, gives the waffles a superb rich color and delicious moistness.

2 cups	sifted cake-and-pastry flour	500 mL
⅓ cup	chopped toasted pecans (optional)	75 mL
4 tsp	baking powder	20 mL
¼ tsp	salt	1 mL
2	eggs, separated	2
1½ cups	milk	375 mL
1 cup	puréed cooked sweet potato	250 mL
⅓ cup	butter, melted	75 mL
2 tsp	grated orange rind	10 mL
1 tbsp	granulated sugar	15 mL

- In large bowl, combine flour, pecans (if using), baking powder and salt. Whisk together egg yolks, milk, sweet potato, butter and orange rind; pour over dry ingredients. Stir together just until moistened.

- In separate bowl, beat egg whites until soft peaks form; beat in sugar until stiff peaks form. Stir about half into potato mixture; fold in remainder.

- Using ⅓ cup (75 mL) for each waffle, pour onto heated nonstick or lightly greased waffle iron; cover and cook for 4 to 5 minutes or until golden brown and waffle iron stops steaming. (Or cook in lightly greased skillet for about 3 minutes per side or until puffed and golden brown.)

Makes 12 waffles.

PER WAFFLE: about 165 calories, 4 g protein, 7 g fat, 21 g carbohydrate.

Cape Breton Pancakes

From the Markland by the Sea restaurant in Cape Breton comes this recipe for light and fruity pancakes, which they serve with local maple syrup.

2	eggs	2
¾ cup	plain yogurt	175 mL
½ cup	milk	125 mL
½ cup	apple juice	125 mL
¼ cup	vegetable oil	50 mL
¼ cup	liquid honey	50 mL
1½ cups	all-purpose flour	375 mL
1½ tsp	baking soda	7 mL
½ tsp	salt	2 mL
¼ tsp	cinnamon	1 mL
1	each apple and pear, chopped	1

- In large bowl, whisk together eggs, yogurt, milk, apple juice, oil and honey. Stir together flour, baking soda, salt and cinnamon; sprinkle over egg mixture. Scatter apple and pear over top; stir just until dry ingredients are moistened.

- Heat greased griddle over medium heat. Using 3 tbsp (50 mL) batter for each pancake, drop batter onto griddle; cook for about 3 minutes or until bottom is golden and bubbles break on top but do not fill in. Turn and cook until bottom is golden brown.

Makes 24 pancakes.

PER SERVING OF 4 PANCAKES: about 335 calories, 8 g protein, 13 g fat, 49 g carbohydrate.

Poached Eggs with Ham and Veggie Hash

Ham and eggs seen through new eyes makes a great all-day breakfast. This new light version uses lean ham, very little oil and plenty of vegetables.

2 tsp	vegetable oil	10 mL
¼ lb	smoked ham, turkey or chicken, diced	125 g
1	potato, peeled and diced	1
1	small onion, chopped	1
¼ cup	chicken or vegetable stock	50 mL
¼ tsp	hot pepper sauce (optional)	1 mL
Half	sweet green pepper, chopped	Half
½ cup	corn kernels	125 mL
1	small tomato, diced	1
2	eggs	2
	Chopped fresh parsley	

- In 7-inch (18 cm) nonstick skillet, heat oil over medium-high heat; cook ham, potato and onion, stirring often, for 3 minutes or until onion is softened.

- Add stock, and hot pepper sauce (if using); cover and cook over medium heat for 5 minutes or until potatoes are almost tender. Stir in green pepper, corn and tomato.

- Make 2 nests in mixture; crack egg into each. Cook, covered, for 5 minutes or until eggs are set. Place egg on each plate; surround with vegetables. Sprinkle with parsley.

Makes 2 servings.

PER SERVING: about 355 calories, 23 g protein, 14 g fat, 29 g carbohydrate, good source iron.

Scrambled Egg Burrito

Even in Texas they don't make a better breakfast burrito than this one. Serve with sliced avocado or guacamole.

1 tbsp	vegetable oil	15 mL
½ cup	sliced mushrooms	125 mL
2	green onions, sliced	2
4	eggs, lightly beaten	4
¼ tsp	salt	1 mL
Pinch	pepper	Pinch
½ cup	shredded Cheddar cheese	125 mL
¼ cup	mild salsa or ketchup	50 mL
4	8-inch (20 cm) flour tortillas, warmed	4

- In skillet, heat oil over medium heat; cook mushrooms and onions, stirring, for 2 minutes or until softened.

- Add eggs, salt and pepper; cook, stirring, for 2 to 3 minutes or until almost set. Stir in half of the cheese.

- Evenly spread salsa over each tortilla, leaving 1-inch (2.5 cm) border; divide egg mixture over salsa. Sprinkle with remaining cheese and roll up.

Makes 4 servings.

PER SERVING: about 305 calories, 14 g protein, 16 g fat, 27 g carbohydrate, good source calcium and iron.

Rocky Mountain Eggs

Toronto caterer and outdoors aficionado Ellen Cornwall gets a good start to her camping days with this original version of egg-in-a-hole.

4	slices dense rye bread	4
1 tbsp	butter	15 mL
4	eggs	4
4	slices smoked ham	4
¾ cup	shredded old Cheddar cheese	175 mL
	Pepper	
¼ cup	salsa	50 mL

- Cut 2½-inch (6 cm) round hold in centre of each bread slice. In large nonstick skillet, melt butter over medium heat; place bread in skillet, in batches if necessary. Break 1 egg into each hole; cook for 2 minutes.

- Using spatula, turn bread and egg over; top with ham, cheese, and pepper to taste. Cover and cook for 5 minutes or until cheese is melted and bread is crispy. Serve garnished with salsa.

Makes 4 servings.

PER SERVING: about 290 calories, 19 g protein, 18 g fat, 12 g carbohydrate, good source calcium.

Tomato Cucumber Salsa

Serve this fresh, chunky relish with eggs, hash browns or pan-fried fish.

2	plum tomatoes	2
1	jalapeño pepper, seeded and finely chopped	1
1	green onion, chopped	1
⅓ cup	chopped seeded peeled cucumber	75 mL
1 tbsp	chopped fresh coriander or parsley	15 mL
2 tsp	lime juice	10 mL
½ tsp	minced garlic	2 mL
	Salt	

- Core, seed and chop tomatoes. In bowl, combine tomatoes, jalapeño pepper, onion, cucumber, coriander, lime juice and garlic; season with salt to taste.

Makes about 1⅓ cups (325 mL).

PER ¼ CUP (50 mL): about 8 calories, trace protein and fat, 2 g carbohydrate.

Pineapple Breakfast Pizza

Canada via Hawaii and Italy — here's an easy version of a fruit, tomato, cheese and sausage pizza kids adore.

8	slices whole wheat bread	8
½ cup	tomato sauce	125 mL
½ tsp	dried oregano	2 mL
1½ cups	shredded mozzarella cheese	375 mL
⅔ cup	sliced smoked sausage or diced ham	150 mL
⅔ cup	drained pineapple tidbits	150 mL

- Snugly fit bread into greased 15- x 10-inch (40 x 25 cm) jelly roll pan; bake in 425°F (220°C) oven for 10 minutes or until toasted.

- Spread tomato sauce over toast; sprinkle with oregano, then half of the cheese. Arrange sausage over top; sprinkle with pineapple.

- Sprinkle with remaining cheese; bake for 10 minutes or until melted. Cut in half diagonally to serve.

Makes 8 servings.

PER SERVING: about 180 calories, 9 g protein, 8 g fat, 18 g carbohydrate.

Saucy Smoked Fish

Maritimers know a thing or two about good breakfasts that celebrate their Atlantic catch. Here's a rib sticker from Nova Scotia's Liscombe Lodge, a resort serving one of the finest breakfasts in Canada.

1 lb	smoked cod fillets, cut in 4	500 g
2½ cups	milk	625 mL
¼ cup	butter	50 mL
1	small onion, chopped	1
2 tbsp	all-purpose flour	25 mL
Pinch	pepper	Pinch
	Chopped fresh parsley	
	Lemon slices	

- In large skillet, cover fish with milk and bring to simmer over low heat; poach for 10 minutes. Remove fish to 8-inch (2 L) square baking dish; strain poaching liquid, reserving 1½ cups (375 mL).

- In saucepan, melt butter over medium heat; cook onion, stirring occasionally, for 3 minutes or until softened. Reduce heat to low. Stir in flour; cook, stirring, for 3 minutes without browning. Whisk in reserved poaching liquid and pepper; cook, stirring, for 5 minutes or until thickened and smooth.

- Pour sauce over fillets; bake in 350°F (180°C) oven for 15 minutes or until bubbly. Garnish with parsley and lemon slices.

Makes 4 servings.

PER SERVING: about 265 calories, 24 g protein, 14 g fat, 9 g carbohydrate.

Lemon Scone Hearts

Hot scones for breakfast. Flaky scones for tea. Enjoy this heritage recipe in a new heart-warming shape!

2¼ cups	all-purpose flour	550 mL
2 tbsp	granulated sugar	25 mL
2½ tsp	baking powder	12 mL
2 tsp	grated lemon rind	10 mL
½ tsp	baking soda	2 mL
½ tsp	salt	2 mL
½ cup	cold butter, cubed	125 mL
1 cup	buttermilk	250 mL
1	egg, lightly beaten	1

- In large bowl, combine flour, sugar, baking powder, lemon rind, baking soda and salt. With pastry blender or 2 knives, cut in butter until in coarse crumbs. With fork, stir in buttermilk to make soft slightly sticky dough.

- Turn out onto lightly floured surface; press into ball. Knead gently 10 times. Pat out dough into ¾-inch (2 cm) thick round. Using heart-shaped or round cookie cutter, cut out shapes; place on ungreased baking sheet. Gather up scraps and repat dough once; cut out shapes.

- Brush tops with egg; bake in 425°F (220°C) oven for 12 to 15 minutes or until puffed and golden. Transfer to racks; let cool.

Makes about 12 scones.
PER SCONE: about 170 calories, 4 g protein, 8 g fat, 20 g carbohydrate.

TIP: When serving scones with savory dishes, omit lemon rind.

Peaches and Cream Muffins

Niagara and Okanagan peaches are first-rate, tasting like peaches, not like the cardboard fuzz balls imported out of season. Eat plenty of them fresh and pop a few into muffins.

2 cups	all-purpose flour	500 mL
¾ cup	granulated sugar	175 mL
2 tsp	baking powder	10 mL
¾ tsp	each nutmeg and cinnamon	4 mL
½ tsp	each baking soda and salt	2 mL
1 cup	sour cream	250 mL
2	eggs	2
¼ cup	butter, melted	50 mL
1 tsp	vanilla	5 mL
1 cup	chopped peeled peaches	250 mL
¼ cup	sliced almonds	50 mL

- In large bowl, combine flour, sugar, baking powder, nutmeg, cinnamon, baking soda and salt. Whisk together sour cream, eggs, butter and vanilla; pour over dry ingredients. Pour peaches over top; stir just until dry ingredients are moistened.

- Spoon into greased or paper-lined muffin cups; sprinkle with almonds. Bake in 400°F (200°C) oven for about 20 minutes or until golden and tops are firm to the touch.

Makes 12 muffins.
PER MUFFIN: about 225 calories, 4 g protein, 9 g fat, 32 g carbohydrate.

Carrot Date Breakfast Bars

Carrots are too good and healthy to munch up solely as a side dish. These nouveau muffin bars provide inspiration and lots of beta-carotene.

¾ cup	each all-purpose and whole wheat flours	175 mL
2 tsp	baking powder	10 mL
1½ tsp	cinnamon	7 mL
1 tsp	baking soda	5 mL
1 cup	dates, chopped	250 mL
2	eggs	2
½ cup	packed brown sugar	125 mL
½ cup	vegetable oil	125 mL
2 cups	grated carrot	500 mL

- In large bowl, combine all-purpose and whole wheat flours, baking powder, cinnamon and baking soda; stir in dates. In separate bowl, whisk together eggs, sugar and oil; stir in carrot. Pour over dry ingredients; stir just until combined.

- Spread in greased 8-inch (2 L) square cake pan; bake in 350°F (180°C) oven for 45 to 50 minutes or until cake tester inserted in centre comes out clean. Let cool in pan on rack before cutting into squares.

Makes 12 squares.
Per square: about 225 calories, 3 g protein, 10 g fat, 32 g carbohydrate.

Raspberry Oatmeal Muffins

Our test kitchen director, Daphna Rabinovitch, trained as a pastry chef. Her expertise shines in breakfast bakes such as these berry-in-every-bite muffins.

1¼ cups	all-purpose flour	300 mL
1 cup	rolled oats (not instant)	250 mL
⅓ cup	packed brown sugar	75 mL
1 tsp	cinnamon	5 mL
1 tsp	each baking powder and baking soda	5 mL
1 cup	buttermilk	250 mL
⅓ cup	vegetable oil	75 mL
2 tbsp	molasses	25 mL
1	egg	1
1 tsp	vanilla	5 mL
1½ cups	fresh raspberries	375 mL

- In large bowl, combine flour, oats, brown sugar, cinnamon, baking powder and baking soda. Whisk together buttermilk, oil, molasses, egg and vanilla; pour over dry ingredients. Sprinkle with raspberries; gently stir just until dry ingredients are moistened.

- Spoon into greased or paper-lined muffin cups, filling three-quarters full. Bake in 375°F (190°C) oven for about 20 minutes or until tops are firm to the touch.

Makes 10 muffins.
Per muffin: about 220 calories, 5 g protein, 9 g fat, 31 g carbohydrate.

Light Strawberry Jam

In the pursuit of lower sugar jams, the test kitchen created this quartet of fruit spreads. They have a softer set than jams set with pectin, but the old-fashioned fruit flavor is right there.

8 cups	halved strawberries	2 L
1 cup	granulated sugar	250 mL
½ cup	corn syrup	125 mL
2 tbsp	lemon juice	25 mL

• In large heavy nonaluminum saucepan and using potato masher, crush half of the strawberries. Add remaining strawberries and ½ cup (125 mL) water; bring to boil over medium heat. Reduce heat to medium-low; cover and simmer for 10 minutes.

PRESERVING TIPS

TESTING FOR SET

• Place 2 small plates in freezer to chill. Drop ½ tsp (2 mL) hot jam onto 1 chilled plate and let cool. Return to freezer for 2 minutes. Tilt plate; if jam flows slowly, it has reached appropriate thickness for softly set jam. If it remains syrupy, continue to boil jam, repeating test every few minutes until jam is softly set, always using coldest clean plate.

PREPARING EQUIPMENT

• About 30 minutes before filling jars, fill boiling water bath canner two-thirds full of water. Bring to boil.
• Use only new lids and canning jars free of nicks.
• Wash, rinse and air-dry jars. Fifteen minutes before filling, place jars, funnel and ½ cup (125 mL) metal measure in canner rack; boil for 15 minutes.
• Boil new canning lids with jars for last 5 minutes.

PROCESSING JAM

• Fill jars, using funnel and metal measure for ladling, leaving recommended headspace. Avoid splashing jam onto rim of jar; wipe rim if necessary.
• Centre lids on jars; screw on bands fingertip-tight.
• Place jars in rack; lower into canner. Pour in enough boiling water to cover jars by 2 inches (5 cm). Cover and return to boil; boil for recommended time.
• Let jars cool on rack for 24 hours. Check that lids curve downward. (If any don't, refrigerate to use within 3 weeks.) Label and store in cool, dry, dark place for up to 1 year.

• Stir in sugar, corn syrup and lemon juice; return to boil and boil vigorously, uncovered and stirring almost constantly, for 15 to 20 minutes or just until softly set (see Preserving Tips). Remove from heat. Using metal spoon, skim off any foam.

• Ladle into hot canning jars, leaving ¼-inch (5 mm) headspace. Seal jars; process in boiling water bath for 10 minutes. Let cool on racks. Store in cool, dry, dark place for up to 4 months. Once opened, store in refrigerator for up to 4 weeks.

Makes about 4 cups (1 L).
PER TBSP (15 mL): about 25 calories, trace protein and fat, 6 g carbohydrate.

VARIATIONS
• RASPBERRY: Substitute whole raspberries for strawberries. Omit lemon juice.
• PEACH APRICOT: Substitute 4 cups (1 L) each chopped peeled peaches and apricots for strawberries; reduce lemon juice to 1 tbsp (15 mL).
• PLUM: Substitute chopped unpeeled plums for strawberries. Reduce lemon juice to 1 tbsp (15 mL).

Peach Apricot Smoothie

Even out of season you can get the benefits of apricots and peaches. Just use the canned variety, but look for fruit preserved in juice rather than in syrup.

1 cup	milk	250 mL
1	can (14 oz/398 mL) peach halves, drained	1
½ cup	drained canned apricot halves	125 mL
1 tbsp	lemon juice	15 mL
1 tsp	liquid honey	5 mL
Pinch	cinnamon	Pinch

• In blender, combine milk, peaches, apricots, lemon juice, honey and cinnamon; purée until thick and frothy.

Makes 4 servings.
PER SERVING: about 95 calories, 3 g protein, 1 g fat, 20 g carbohydrate.

Strawberry Banana Smoothie

Who needs an ice-cream shake when banana adds body to a breakfast drink? This one is fragrant with vitamin C–rich strawberries and is based on an all-important calcium source — milk.

2 cups	sliced strawberries (fresh or thawed)	500 mL
1 cup	milk	250 mL
1	banana	1
1 tbsp	lemon juice	15 mL
1 tbsp	liquid honey	15 mL
Pinch	cinnamon	Pinch

• In blender, combine strawberries, milk, banana, lemon juice, honey and cinnamon; purée until thick and frothy.

Makes 2 servings.
PER SERVING: about 195 calories, 6 g protein, 3 g fat, 39 g carbohydrate, high source fibre, good source calcium.

CHAPTER NINE

SWEET SENSATIONS

*There's no denying the
Canadian sweet tooth.
Now, because we are all more
health-conscious, dessert
must be worth every calorie.
Here are some fine
temptations for those times
you treat yourself.*

Almond Baked Apples

The simplest dishes are often the most memorable. These honeyed almond-and-cranberry-stuffed apples add a contemporary touch to an old favorite.

½ cup	apple juice	125 mL
⅓ cup	liquid honey	75 mL
2 tbsp	butter	25 mL
¼ tsp	nutmeg	1 mL
4	tart baking apples	4
¼ cup	dried cranberries or raisins	50 mL
3 tbsp	toasted slivered almonds	50 mL
3 tbsp	cookie crumbs (ginger, sugar, graham)	50 mL

- In small saucepan, combine apple juice, honey, butter and nutmeg; bring to boil. Reduce heat and boil gently for 10 to 12 minutes or until thickened.

- Meanwhile, core apples almost to bottom, leaving base intact. Pare off ¾-inch (2 cm) wide strip around core at top; trim base to make level if necessary. Place in 8-inch (2 L) square baking dish.

- Pour juice mixture over apples. Cover and bake in 375°F (190°C) oven for about 45 minutes or until tender, basting twice.

- Combine cranberries, almonds and cookie crumbs; stuff into apple cavities. Baste with pan juices; bake for 5 minutes longer. Baste again before serving.

Makes 4 servings.
PER SERVING: about 330 calories, 2 g protein, 10 g fat, 63 g carbohydrate, high source fibre.

TIP: The old fruit-and-cream combo is hard to beat, but whipping cream and high-fat ice cream have been lightened up of late. At *Canadian Living*, we like to drain low-fat yogurt in a cheesecloth-lined sieve set over a bowl in the refrigerator. The longer it drains, the thicker the yogurt becomes (from 4 to 12 hours is good). This "creamy" sauce can be sweetened if desired and accented with lemon or orange rind. Or, if you insist, mix it with equal amounts of lightly whipped cream. Thickened yogurt is now available in many markets. Use it the way you would high-fat alternatives.

Deep-Dish Peach Crisp

When peaches are ripe and juicy, who can resist the warm comfort of a just-baked crisp? The spicy crunch of an easy cookie streusel gives this old favorite a new snap.

8 cups	sliced peeled peaches (about 8 large peaches)	2 L
¼ cup	granulated sugar	50 mL
2 tsp	cornstarch	10 mL
1 cup	gingersnap cookie crumbs	250 mL
½ cup	all-purpose flour	125 mL
⅓ cup	packed brown sugar	75 mL
3 tbsp	butter	50 mL

- In large bowl, toss together peaches, sugar and cornstarch; arrange in 8-inch (2 L) square baking dish.

- In separate bowl, combine cookie crumbs, flour and sugar; cut in butter until crumbly. Sprinkle over peach mixture.

- Bake in 375°F (190°C) oven for 40 to 45 minutes or until bubbly and golden brown. Let stand for 30 minutes.

Makes 8 servings.
Per serving: about 285 calories, 3 g protein, 6 g fat, 56 g carbohydrate.

Tip: To peel peaches easily, cut shallow X in skin at bottom of fruit. Immerse in boiling water for 1 minute. Using slotted spoon, transfer peaches to bowl of cold water. When cool enough to handle, pull skins off with paring knife.

Summer Fruit Sauté

Cooks will find it hard to resist sampling this tantalizing medley of fruits as they soften and mellow with cinnamon and vanilla. Spoon over angel food cake or a mound of ice cream.

¼ cup	apple juice or peach nectar	50 mL
2 tbsp	packed brown sugar	25 mL
1 tbsp	butter	15 mL
1 tsp	vanilla	5 mL
Pinch	cinnamon	Pinch
2	apricots, quartered	2
2	red plums, sliced	2
1	nectarine, sliced	1
1 cup	raspberries	250 mL

- In saucepan, combine apple juice, sugar, butter, vanilla and cinnamon; cook over medium-high heat just until bubbly.

- Stir in apricots, plums and nectarine; cook, stirring gently, for 2 to 3 minutes or just until fruit is slightly softened. Remove from heat; stir in raspberries. Serve immediately or let cool to room temperature.

Makes 4 servings.
Per serving: about 120 calories, 1 g protein, 3 g fat, 23 g carbohydrate.

Bananas in Caramel Sauce

This is a quick dessert to make at the last minute and spoon over ice cream. You can make the sauce ahead of time, then add and heat the bananas just before serving.

½ cup	granulated sugar	125 mL
2 tbsp	water	25 mL
½ cup	pineapple or orange juice	125 mL
2 tbsp	butter	25 mL
3 tbsp	rum	50 mL
1 tbsp	lemon juice	15 mL
½ tsp	cinnamon	2 mL
6	bananas	6
6	small scoops vanilla ice cream	6

- In large deep skillet, heat sugar with water over medium heat, watching carefully, until sugar melts and starts to turn caramel color. Gently stir in pineapple juice and butter, being careful because mixture will bubble up.

- Add rum, lemon juice and cinnamon; cook, stirring, for 4 to 5 minutes or until smooth. *(Sauce can be cooled, covered and refrigerated for up to 12 hours; reheat gently.)*

- Cut bananas into 1-inch (2.5 cm) thick slices; add to sauce and heat through. Serve over ice cream.

Makes 6 servings.
PER SERVING: about 295 calories, 3 g protein, 8 g fat, 54 g carbohydrate.

Kay Spicer's Crunchy Seed Cookies

Writer, author and authority on cooking healthfully, Kay Spicer likens these rolled cookies to an English biscuit and suggests pairing them with cheese.

⅓ cup	butter	75 mL
½ cup	packed brown sugar	125 mL
1	egg	1
1 tsp	vanilla	5 mL
½ cup	all-purpose flour	125 mL
½ cup	whole wheat flour	125 mL
½ cup	wheat germ	125 mL
¼ cup	oat bran	50 mL
1 tsp	cinnamon	5 mL
½ tsp	salt	2 mL
2 tbsp	each sunflower, sesame and poppy seeds	25 mL

- In bowl, beat butter with sugar until light and fluffy; beat in egg and vanilla.

- Mix together all-purpose and whole wheat flours, wheat germ, oat bran, cinnamon and salt; stir into butter mixture, mixing well. Stir in sunflower, sesame and poppy seeds.

- Between 2 sheets of waxed paper, roll out dough, in batches, to ⅛-inch (3 mm) thickness. With cookie cutter, cut into 2½-inch (6 cm) rounds; place on ungreased baking sheets. Bake in 350°F (180°C) oven for 8 to 10 minutes or until lightly browned. Let cool on baking sheets for 5 minutes; transfer to racks and let cool completely.

Makes 48 cookies.
PER COOKIE: about 42 calories, 1 g protein, 2 g fat, 5 g carbohydrate.

Daphna Rabinovitch's Fudgy Chocolate Raspberry Brownies

Test kitchen director Daphna Rabinovitch serves these chocolaty brownies very simply with a sprinkle of icing sugar or, for swish occasions, with a raspberry sauce and a few raspberries.

1 cup	packed raspberries (fresh or thawed)	250 mL
4 oz	unsweetened chocolate, chopped	125 g
½ cup	unsalted butter, cubed	125 mL
3	eggs	3
1¼ cups	granulated sugar	300 mL
½ tsp	vanilla	2 mL
¾ cup	all-purpose flour	175 mL
1 tsp	icing sugar	5 mL

- In food processor or blender, purée raspberries; pass through fine sieve to remove seeds. Set aside.

- In top of double boiler over hot (not boiling) water, melt chocolate with butter; let cool slightly.

- In bowl, beat eggs with sugar for about 5 minutes or until pale and thickened. On low speed, beat in vanilla and chocolate mixture; beat in raspberry purée. With wooden spoon, stir in flour.

- Scrape batter into greased 9-inch (2.5 L) square cake pan. Bake in 350°F (180°C) oven for 25 to 30 minutes or until cake tester inserted in centre still has moist crumbs clinging to it. Let cool completely in pan on rack. Sprinkle with icing sugar. Cut into squares. *(Squares can be covered and stored in refrigerator for up to 5 days or frozen in airtight container for up to 1 month.)*

Makes 16 squares.
PER SQUARE: about 190 calories, 3 g protein, 11 g fat, 23 g carbohydrate.

Cappuccino Nanaimo Bars

It's fascinating to see how a traditional bar can blossom with all kinds of delectable variations such as this coffee one.

½ cup	unsalted butter	125 mL
⅓ cup	unsweetened cocoa powder	75 mL
¼ cup	granulated sugar	50 mL
1	egg, lightly beaten	1
1½ cups	graham cracker crumbs	375 mL
1 cup	shredded coconut	250 mL
½ cup	finely chopped walnuts	125 mL
FILLING:		
2 tbsp	milk	25 mL
3 tbsp	unsalted butter	50 mL
2 tsp	instant espresso powder or coffee granules	10 mL
½ tsp	vanilla	2 mL
2 cups	icing sugar	500 mL
TOPPING:		
4 oz	semisweet chocolate, coarsely chopped	125 g
1 tbsp	unsalted butter	15 mL
½ tsp	instant espresso powder	2 mL

- In heavy saucepan, combine butter, cocoa, sugar and egg; cook over low heat, stirring, until butter is melted. Remove from heat; stir in graham cracker crumbs, coconut and walnuts.

- Pat evenly into greased 9-inch (2.5 L) square cake pan. Bake in 350°F (180°C) oven for 10 to 12 minutes or until just firm. Let cool completely on rack.

- FILLING: In small saucepan, heat milk, butter, espresso powder and vanilla over low heat until butter is melted and espresso powder is dissolved. Transfer to mixing bowl; let cool. Beat in sugar until thickened and smooth; spread evenly over cooled base. Refrigerate for about 45 minutes or until firm.

- TOPPING: Meanwhile, in top of double boiler over hot (not boiling) water, melt together chocolate, butter and espresso powder; spread over filling. With sharp knife, score topping only into bars. Refrigerate until topping is set. Cut into bars. *(Bars can be covered and refrigerated for up to 5 days or frozen in airtight container for up to 1 month.)*

Makes 24 bars.
PER BAR: about 190 calories, 2 g protein, 12 g fat, 22 g carbohydrate.

Tart Lemon Squares with Walnut Crust

These squares are impressive nestled in tiny paper cups for elegant occasions.

1 cup	all-purpose flour	250 mL
¼ cup	icing sugar	50 mL
Pinch	salt	Pinch
½ cup	unsalted butter	125 mL
⅓ cup	finely chopped walnuts	75 mL
TOPPING:		
2	eggs	2
¾ cup	granulated sugar	175 mL
1 tbsp	finely grated lemon rind	15 mL
¼ cup	lemon juice	50 mL
2 tbsp	all-purpose flour	25 mL
½ tsp	baking powder	2 mL
1 tsp	icing sugar	5 mL

- In food processor or bowl, blend together flour, icing sugar and salt; pulse or cut in butter with pastry blender until in fine crumbs. Add walnuts. Press handfuls of dough together; pat into greased 8-inch (2 L) square cake pan. Bake in 350°F (180°C) oven for 20 to 25 minutes or until golden. Let cool on rack for 15 minutes.

- TOPPING: Meanwhile, in bowl, beat eggs with sugar until pale and thickened; beat in lemon rind and juice, flour and baking powder. Pour over base; bake for 25 to 30 minutes or until set in centre and golden brown. Let cool on rack. Dust with icing sugar. Cut into squares. *(Squares can be covered and refrigerated for up to 4 days.)*

Makes 20 squares.
PER SQUARE: about 125 calories, 2 g protein, 7 g fat, 15 g carbohydrate.

Hawaiian Bars

Transport yourself to the Pacific with these tropical bars, lush with dried fruit and macadamia nuts.

½ cup	unsalted butter, softened	125 mL
¾ cup	packed brown sugar	175 mL
2 tsp	white vinegar	10 mL
1 tsp	vanilla	5 mL
2 cups	all-purpose flour	500 mL
Pinch	salt	Pinch
TOPPING:		
3	eggs	3
¾ cup	packed brown sugar	175 mL
1 tsp	vanilla	5 mL
2 cups	flaked coconut	500 mL
1 cup	each chopped dried pineapple and papaya	250 mL
1 cup	chopped lightly salted macadamia nuts	250 mL

Photo (clockwise from top): Cappuccino Nanaimo Bars; Hawaiian Bars; Tart Lemon Squares with Walnut Crust

- Lightly grease 13- x 9-inch (3.5 L) cake pan; line with foil, leaving 2-inch (5 cm) overhang on each long side.

- In bowl, beat butter with sugar; beat in vinegar and vanilla. With wooden spoon, gradually stir in flour and salt until dough is crumbly. Lightly knead portions of dough together; press into prepared pan. Bake in 350°F (180°C) oven for 15 to 20 minutes or until lightly browned. Let cool on rack for 15 minutes.

- TOPPING: In bowl, beat together eggs, sugar and vanilla for about 2 minutes or until smooth; stir in coconut, pineapple, papaya and nuts. Pour over crust, smoothing top; bake for 30 to 35 minutes longer or until topping is lightly browned. Let cool completely on rack.

- With knife, cut along ends of pan; using foil overhang, loosen from pan. Invert onto back of baking sheet; peel off foil. Invert onto board; cut into bars. *(Bars can be refrigerated in airtight container for up to 5 days or frozen for up to 1 month.)*

Makes 32 bars.

PER BAR: about 175 calories, 2 g protein, 8 g fat, 26 g carbohydrate.

La Grange Maple Sugar Apple Pie

Regional cooking is thriving in Quebec, as this creamy apple and maple sugar specialty of the Restaurant La Grange de St-Charles in the town of St-Charles-sur-Richelieu attests.

1½ cups	packed brown sugar or granulated maple sugar	375 mL
½ cup	evaporated milk	125 mL
¼ cup	water	50 mL
⅓ cup	all-purpose flour	75 mL
3 tbsp	butter, softened	50 mL
1	egg	1
4 cups	thinly sliced peeled apples	1 L
1	unbaked 9-inch (23 cm) single-crust pie shell	1
½ cup	chopped walnuts	125 mL

- In saucepan, stir together sugar, milk and water over medium heat until dissolved; let cool.

- In bowl, beat flour with butter; beat in egg until smooth. Gradually beat in sugar mixture. Add apples, tossing to coat well. Spoon into pie shell; sprinkle with walnuts.

- Bake in 425°F (220°C) oven for 15 minutes; reduce heat to 350°F (180°C) and bake for 40 to 45 minutes longer or until apples are tender and filling is set. Let cool on rack.

Makes 8 to 10 servings.

PER EACH OF 10 SERVINGS: about 345 calories, 4 g protein, 14 g fat, 52 g carbohydrate.

Silver Spoon Butterscotch Peach Pie

From Halifax's The Silver Spoon Restaurant and Dessert Cafe comes just one of the 250 different kinds of desserts owner Deanna Silver creates from scratch in a year.

	Pastry for 9-inch (23 cm) double-crust pie	
6 cups	sliced peeled peaches (6 large)	1.5 L
1 tbsp	lemon juice	15 mL
¼ cup	butter	50 mL
½ cup	packed brown sugar	125 mL
2 tbsp	all-purpose flour	25 mL
Pinch	salt	Pinch

CANADIAN LIVING'S PERFECT PASTRY

In bowl, mix 3 cups (750 mL) all-purpose flour with 1 tsp (5 mL) salt; cut in ½ cup (125 mL) each butter and lard or shortening. Beat together 1 egg, 2 tsp (10 mL) vinegar and enough ice water to make ⅔ cup (150 mL); sprinkle over top and toss until dough holds together. Press into 2 discs. Wrap and refrigerate for at least 30 minutes or up to 3 days. Makes enough for 1 double-crust 9- or 10-inch (23 or 25 cm) pie.

- On lightly floured surface, roll out half of the pastry and fit into 9-inch (23 cm) pie plate; set aside.

- In bowl, combine peaches with lemon juice; set aside. In saucepan, melt butter over medium heat; stir in sugar just until blended, about 30 seconds. Remove from heat; stir in flour and salt. Stir into peaches; spoon into pie shell.

- Roll out remaining pastry. Using fluted pastry wheel or knife, cut into ¾-inch (2 cm) wide strips. Moisten pastry rim. Weave strips over filling, pressing ends firmly to rim; trim and crimp edge.

- Bake in 425°F (220°C) oven for 15 minutes; reduce heat to 350°F (180°C) and bake for 35 minutes longer or until pastry is golden and filling bubbly. Let cool on rack.

Makes 6 to 8 servings.

PER EACH OF 8 SERVINGS: about 370 calories, 4 g protein, 19 g fat, 47 g carbohydrate.

Clockwise from top: La Grange Maple Sugar Apple Pie; Silver Spoon Butterscotch Peach Pie; Wanda's Pie in the Sky Ambrosia; A la Mode Bumbleberry Pie

Wanda's Pie in the Sky Ambrosia

With high fluting, wide-lattice tops and creative combinations of fruits, Wanda Beaver, owner of Wanda's Pie in the Sky in Toronto, has made old-fashioned pies a form of art.

	Pastry for 10-inch (25 cm) double-crust pie	
5 cups	sliced peeled peaches (about 5)	1.25 L
1½ cups	sliced peeled apples	375 mL
1 cup	raspberries	250 mL
1 cup	blueberries	250 mL
1 tbsp	lemon juice	15 mL
¼ tsp	almond extract	1 mL
1 cup	granulated sugar	250 mL
2 tbsp	chopped pecans	25 mL
¼ cup	cornstarch	50 mL
Pinch	cinnamon	Pinch
1	egg yolk	1
1 tsp	water	5 mL

- On lightly floured surface, roll out half of the pastry and fit into 10-inch (25 cm) pie plate; set aside.

- In bowl, toss together peaches, apples, raspberries, blueberries, lemon juice and almond extract. Toss 2 tbsp (25 mL) of the sugar with pecans; set aside. Combine remaining sugar, cornstarch and cinnamon; toss gently with fruit mixture. Spoon into pie shell.

- Roll out remaining pastry. Using fluted pastry wheel or knife, cut into 1½-inch (4 cm) wide strips. Moisten pastry rim. Weave strips tightly over filling, pressing ends firmly to rim; trim and crimp edge. Mix egg yolk with water; brush over pastry. Sprinkle with pecan mixture.

- Bake in 425°F (220°C) oven for 15 minutes; reduce heat to 350°F (180°C) and bake for 40 minutes longer or until pastry is golden and filling bubbly. Let cool on rack.

Makes 8 to 10 servings.
PER EACH OF 10 SERVINGS: about 365 calories, 4 g protein, 15 g fat, 56 g carbohydrate.

A la Mode Bumbleberry Pie

You know you're getting close to A la Mode in Vancouver's Granville Island Public Market when you pass people balancing cappuccinos and juicy wedges of pie topped with ice cream (à la mode).

	Pastry for 9-inch (23 cm) double-crust pie	
1 cup	chopped rhubarb	250 mL
2 cups	chopped peeled apples	500 mL
1 cup	blackberries	250 mL
1 cup	raspberries	250 mL
¾ cup	granulated sugar	175 mL
4 tsp	all-purpose flour	20 mL
4 tsp	cornstarch	20 mL
4 tsp	butter	20 mL
1 tbsp	lemon juice	15 mL

- On lightly floured surface, roll out half of the pastry and fit into 9-inch (23 cm) pie plate; set aside.

- In microwaveable measure, microwave rhubarb at High for 50 seconds or until slightly softened. (Or place in steamer and steam for 3 minutes.)

- In large bowl, combine rhubarb, apples, blackberries and raspberries. Combine sugar, flour and cornstarch; toss gently with fruit mixture. Spoon into pie shell; dot with butter and sprinkle with lemon juice.

- Roll out remaining pastry; moisten rim of pastry shell and fit pastry over filling, pressing gently to rim. Trim and crimp edge; cut steam vents in top.

- Bake in 425°F (220°C) oven for 15 minutes; reduce heat to 350°F (180°C) and bake for 35 minutes or until pastry is golden and filling bubbly. Let cool on rack.

Makes 6 to 8 servings.
PER EACH OF 8 SERVINGS: about 340 calories, 3 g protein, 16 g fat, 47 g carbohydrate.

Rustic Rhubarb Tart

Baked without the confines of a pie plate, this "free-form" tart owes its inspiration to French country bakeries.

6 cups	chopped rhubarb	1.5 L
1 cup	granulated sugar	250 mL
¼ cup	all-purpose flour	50 mL
¼ tsp	nutmeg	1 mL
¼ cup	coarsely chopped pecans	50 mL
1 tbsp	milk	15 mL
	Icing sugar	
PASTRY:		
3 cups	all-purpose flour	750 mL
¼ cup	granulated sugar	50 mL
¼ tsp	salt	1 mL
1½ cups	cold butter	375 mL
⅔ cup	cold water	150 mL

- PASTRY: In bowl, combine flour, sugar and salt; using pastry blender or 2 knives, cut in butter until in fine crumbs. Sprinkle with water; stir with fork just until moistened.

- Turn out onto lightly floured surface; knead lightly 5 or 6 times just until dough forms ball. Flatten slightly into disc; wrap and refrigerate for 30 minutes.

- On lightly floured surface, roll out pastry into 16-inch (40 cm) circle, leaving edges rough. Transfer to 12-inch (30 cm) pizza pan, letting pastry hang over edge.

- In bowl, combine rhubarb, sugar, flour and nutmeg; arrange over pastry. Sprinkle with pecans. Fold pastry overhang over filling; brush pastry with milk.

- Bake in 425°F (220°C) oven for 10 minutes. Reduce heat to 375°F (190°C); bake for 35 to 40 minutes longer or until rhubarb is tender and pastry golden. Let cool on rack; dust with icing sugar.

Makes 12 servings.
PER SERVING: about 440 calories, 5 g protein, 25 g fat, 50 g carbohydrate.

Frozen Peanut Butter Pie

This great no-bake make-ahead dessert is pretty wonderful, especially for folks who love those two childhood favorites — chocolate and peanut butter.

1 cup	chocolate cookie crumbs	250 mL
¼ cup	butter, melted	50 mL
FILLING:		
⅔ cup	sour cream	150 mL
3 tbsp	icing sugar	50 mL
2 tbsp	whipping cream	25 mL
⅔ cup	smooth peanut butter	150 mL
TOPPING:		
2 oz	semisweet chocolate, coarsely chopped	60 g
¼ cup	whipping cream	50 mL
¼ cup	chopped peanuts	50 mL

- Stir cookie crumbs with butter until thoroughly moistened; pat onto bottom only of ungreased 9-inch (23 cm) pie plate. Freeze for 20 minutes.

- FILLING: In bowl, whisk together sour cream, sugar and whipping cream; whisk in peanut butter until smooth. Spread evenly over crust. Freeze for 1 hour.

- TOPPING: Meanwhile, in small saucepan, melt chocolate with whipping cream over medium-low heat, stirring until smooth. Let cool for 15 minutes.

- Spread chocolate mixture evenly over filling. Sprinkle peanuts around edge of pie. Freeze for about 1 hour or until completely set. *(Pie can be wrapped, enclosed in rigid airtight container and stored in freezer for up to 1 week.)* Let stand at room temperature for 10 minutes before serving.

Makes 12 servings.
PER SERVING: about 250 calories, 6 g protein, 20 g fat, 14 g carbohydrate.

Lemon Feather Cake

From the kitchen of Mieka Wiens of Regina comes this gluten-free cake as light as the name suggests.

6	eggs, separated	6
1 tbsp	grated lemon rind	15 mL
1¼ cups	instant dissolving (fruit/berry) sugar	300 mL
¾ cup	potato flour or potato starch	175 mL
¼ cup	lemon juice	50 mL
	Icing sugar	
LEMON CREAM FILLING:		
2 tbsp	grated lemon rind	25 mL
½ cup	lemon juice	125 mL
½ cup	granulated sugar	125 mL
¼ cup	butter	50 mL
3	eggs, lightly beaten	3
1 cup	whipping cream	250 mL

- **LEMON CREAM FILLING:** In top of double boiler over simmering water, cook lemon rind and juice, sugar and butter, stirring, until butter is melted. Gradually whisk into eggs.

- Return to top of double boiler; cook, whisking, for about 10 minutes or until thickened. Do not boil. Pour into bowl; place plastic wrap directly on surface. Let cool and refrigerate for at least 8 hours or up to 5 days.

- In large bowl, beat egg yolks, lemon rind and half of the sugar for 5 minutes or until pale and thickened; set aside. In separate bowl and using clean beaters, beat egg whites until soft peaks form; gradually beat in remaining sugar until stiff peaks form.

- Sprinkle one-third of the flour over yolk mixture and fold in; fold in half of the egg whites. Repeat once. Fold in remaining flour. Transfer ¼ cup (50 mL) batter to small bowl; gradually fold in lemon juice. Fold back into remaining batter.

- Pour into parchment paper-lined 10-inch (3 L) springform pan. Bake in 350°F (180°C) oven for 35 to 40 minutes or until tester inserted in centre comes out clean. Let cool on rack; remove pan and paper.

- Whip cream; fold into filling. Using serrated knife, slice cake horizontally. Place bottom layer on plate and spread with filling; top with remaining layer. Sift icing sugar over top.

Makes 10 servings.
PER SERVING: about 370 calories, 7 g protein, 18 g fat, 48 g carbohydrate, good source iron.

Chocolate Orange Torte with Raspberry Coulis

"Coulis" is restaurant talk for sauce, and in the new style of serving, the sauce goes under the cake.

1½ cups	unsalted butter or margarine	375 mL
12 oz	semisweet chocolate, coarsely chopped	375 g
¾ cup	granulated sugar	175 mL
¾ cup	orange juice	175 mL
2 tbsp	orange liqueur (optional)	25 mL
1 tsp	vanilla	5 mL
6	eggs	6
	Unsweetened cocoa powder	
	Raspberries and mint leaves	

RASPBERRY COULIS:

1	pkg (425 g) frozen unsweetened raspberries, thawed	1
1 tbsp	granulated sugar	15 mL
1 tbsp	orange liqueur (optional)	15 mL

- Line bottom of 9-inch (2.5 L) springform pan with parchment paper; set aside.

- In top of double boiler over hot (not boiling) water, melt together butter, chocolate, sugar and orange juice, stirring to blend. Remove from heat; stir in orange liqueur (if using) and vanilla. Let cool.

- Whisk in eggs, 1 at a time. Pour into prepared pan. Bake in 350°F (180°C) oven for 40 to 45 minutes or until edge is slightly crusty and middle is just set. Let cool on rack. Cover with plastic wrap and refrigerate for at least 12 hours or up to 24 hours.

- RASPBERRY COULIS: In food processor, purée raspberries; press through sieve into bowl to remove seeds. Stir in sugar, and orange liqueur (if using).

- Invert cake onto serving platter; remove pan. Sift cocoa powder over top; garnish with raspberries and mint leaves. Slice and serve with raspberry coulis.

Makes 16 servings.
PER SERVING: about 345 calories, 4 g protein, 27 g fat, 27 g carbohydrate.

Yogurt Peach Coffee Cake

Fresh peaches provide a luscious moisture, so you can cut back on the fat that you usually find in a caramel-bottom coffee cake. Like all coffee cakes, this one is best enjoyed the day it's made.

4	large peaches	4
⅓ cup	packed brown sugar	75 mL
1 tbsp	apple juice	15 mL
1 tsp	cinnamon	5 mL
½ cup	butter, softened	125 mL
¾ cup	granulated sugar	175 mL
2	eggs	2
1 tsp	vanilla	5 mL
2 cups	sifted cake-and-pastry flour	500 mL
2 tsp	baking powder	10 mL
1 tsp	baking soda	5 mL
1 tsp	cinnamon	5 mL
¼ tsp	salt	1 mL
1 cup	low-fat plain yogurt	250 mL

- Peel, pit and thickly slice peaches to make 3½ cups (875 mL). In bowl, toss peaches with brown sugar, apple juice and cinnamon; scrape into greased 8½-inch (2.25 L) springform pan, levelling surface as much as possible. Centre pan on large piece of foil; press up tightly to side of pan.

- In separate bowl, beat butter with sugar until light and fluffy; beat in eggs, 1 at a time, beating well after each addition. Beat in vanilla. Combine flour, baking powder, baking soda, cinnamon and salt; stir into butter mixture alternately with yogurt, making 3 additions of dry ingredients and 2 of yogurt. Scrape batter over peach mixture, smoothing evenly.

- Bake on baking sheet in 350°F (180°C) oven for 55 to 60 minutes or until cake tester inserted in centre comes out clean. Let cool in pan on rack for 10 minutes. Run knife around cake and invert onto platter; remove pan.

Makes 10 servings.
PER SERVING: about 310 calories, 5 g protein, 11 g fat, 48 g carbohydrate.

Chocolate Sour Cream Coffee Cake

Let a weekend brunch be the occasion for this tempting cake to serve with fruit.

½ cup	butter, softened	125 mL
1¼ cups	granulated sugar	300 mL
2	eggs	2
1 tsp	vanilla	5 mL
1⅔ cups	all-purpose flour	400 mL
⅓ cup	sifted unsweetened cocoa powder	75 mL
1 tsp	baking powder	5 mL
½ tsp	baking soda	2 mL
½ tsp	salt	2 mL
1 cup	sour cream	250 mL
STREUSEL:		
⅓ cup	packed brown sugar	75 mL
¼ cup	all-purpose flour	50 mL
2 tbsp	butter	25 mL
½ cup	chocolate chips	125 mL
⅓ cup	chopped pecans, toasted	75 mL

- STREUSEL: In bowl, stir together sugar and flour; cut in butter until crumbly. Stir in chocolate chips and pecans; set aside.

- In large bowl, beat butter with sugar until light and fluffy; beat in eggs, 1 at a time. Blend in vanilla. Stir together flour, cocoa, baking powder, baking soda and salt; stir into creamed mixture alternately with sour cream, making 3 additions of dry ingredients and 2 of sour cream.

- Scrape batter into greased 9-inch (2.5 L) springform pan; sprinkle streusel over top. Bake in 350°F (180°C) oven for about 1 hour and 10 minutes or until tester inserted in centre comes out clean. Let cool in pan on rack for 10 minutes; remove side of pan and serve cake warm.

Makes 12 servings.
PER SERVING: about 370 calories, 5 g protein, 19 g fat, 49 g carbohydrate.

Pumpkin Chiffon Cake

This cake freezes well, and with pumpkin pie flavors, it's a great fall weekend dessert.

2¼ cups	sifted cake-and-pastry flour	550 mL
1½ cups	granulated sugar	375 mL
2 tsp	baking powder	10 mL
½ tsp	each salt and cinnamon	2 mL
¼ tsp	each nutmeg and allspice	1 mL
½ cup	vegetable oil	125 mL
5	egg yolks	5
¾ cup	canned pumpkin	175 mL
1 tbsp	grated orange rind	15 mL
⅓ cup	orange juice	75 mL
7	egg whites	7
½ tsp	cream of tartar	2 mL
	Nutmeg Sauce (recipe below)	

- In large bowl, combine flour, ¾ cup (175 mL) of the sugar, baking powder, salt, cinnamon, nutmeg and allspice; make well in centre. Pour in oil, egg yolks, pumpkin, orange rind and juice; beat well. Set aside.

- In separate bowl, beat egg whites with cream of tartar until soft peaks form; gradually beat in remaining sugar until stiff peaks form. Fold into batter in 3 additions. Pour into ungreased 10-inch (4 L) tube pan.

- Bake in 350°F (180°C) oven for 55 to 60 minutes or until top springs back when lightly pressed. Invert pan and let cake hang in pan until cool. Serve with Nutmeg Sauce.

Makes 8 servings.
PER SERVING OF CAKE: about 440 calories, 8 g protein, 17 g fat, 65 g carbohydrate, good source iron.

Nutmeg Sauce

Spoon warm over Pumpkin Chiffon Cake. To serve chilled, thin with a little more cream or milk and drizzle over baked apples, pies or crisps.

3 tbsp	butter	50 mL
3 tbsp	all-purpose flour	50 mL
½ cup	packed brown sugar	125 mL
1 tsp	nutmeg	5 mL
1½ cups	milk	375 mL
2 tbsp	rum (optional)	25 mL
½ cup	whipping cream	125 mL

- In saucepan, melt butter over medium-low heat; blend in flour and cook, stirring, until barely bubbling.

- Add sugar and nutmeg; gradually stir in milk. Cook over medium heat, stirring, until boiling and thickened. Remove from heat; stir in rum (if using). Let cool slightly. Whip cream; fold into sauce.

Makes about 2 cups (500 mL).
PER ¼ CUP (50 mL): about 175 calories, 2 g protein, 11 g fat, 18 g carbohydrate.

FOR GOOD MEASURE

- All-purpose flour does not need to be sifted, but it and all other ingredients used in baking must be measured accurately. Use liquid measures (glass with spout and handle) for milk, oil, juice and other liquids; use dry measures (nesting metal or plastic cups) for flour, sugar, raisins and the like.

- To measure liquids, set measures on counter; fill to desired amount, bending, if necessary, to be level with the measure as you check.

- For all-purpose flour and granulated sugar, spoon from storage container into dry measure, heaping the ingredient. With a knife, sweep the measure level.

- For cake-and-pastry flour, sift or sieve the flour before measuring in the same way as all-purpose flour.

- For brown sugar, pack the measure without straining, levelling off the top.

Berry-Topped Chocolate Torte

Entertain with ease and style. Make the cake part of this dramatic dessert up to two days ahead; spread on the cream and berries close to serving time.

⅔ cup	ground almonds	150 mL
3 tbsp	all-purpose flour	50 mL
Pinch	salt	Pinch
¾ cup	unsalted butter	175 mL
⅓ cup	unsweetened cocoa powder	75 mL
1 cup	granulated sugar	250 mL
3	eggs, separated	3
¼ cup	Grand Marnier or orange juice concentrate	50 mL

TOPPING:

½ cup	whipping cream	125 mL
1½ tsp	Grand Marnier or vanilla	7 mL
3 cups	strawberries, hulled and sliced (or 2 cups/500 mL whole raspberries)	750 mL
	White chocolate curls (optional)	

- Grease 9-inch (2.5 L) springform pan; line bottom with parchment or waxed paper. Set aside.

- In small bowl, combine almonds, flour and salt; set aside. In small saucepan, melt butter over low heat; stir in cocoa and ¾ cup (175 mL) of the sugar. Remove from heat.

- In large bowl, beat egg yolks for about 4 minutes or until thickened; gradually blend in cocoa mixture. Stir in Grand Marnier, then almond mixture.

- In separate bowl, beat egg whites until soft peaks form; gradually beat in remaining sugar until stiff peaks form. Stir a little into chocolate mixture; gently fold in remaining whites.

- Scrape into prepared pan; bake in 375°F (190°C) oven for 25 to 30 minutes or until cake tester inserted in centre comes out slightly moist. Let cool in pan on rack for 10 minutes. Run knife around cake; remove side of pan. Let cool completely. *(Cake can be wrapped and refrigerated for up to 2 days.)*

- TOPPING: Whip cream with Grand Marnier; spread over top of torte. *(Torte can be prepared to this point, covered and refrigerated for up to 2 hours.)*

- To serve, starting at outside rim, arrange strawberries in circle with tips pointing outward; continue in overlapping circles until at centre. (If using raspberries, place upside down all over topping.) Mound white chocolate curls in centre (if using).

Makes 8 servings.
PER SERVING: about 430 calories, 6 g protein, 30 g fat, 39 g carbohydrate.

Charlotte aux Bleuets

The Saguenay-Lac-Saint-Jean region of Quebec is famous for its pearly blueberries. La Maison de la Rivière at La Baie is where this sophisticated dessert originated.

2	pkg (each 200 g) raspberry Swiss rolls, thinly sliced	2
4 tsp	unflavored gelatin	20 mL
2½ cups	milk	625 mL
1 tsp	vanilla	5 mL
8	egg yolks	8
1 cup	granulated sugar	250 mL
1 cup	whipping cream	250 mL
1 cup	sour cream	250 mL
1 cup	blueberries (fresh or thawed)	250 mL
GARNISH:		
¾ cup	whipping cream	175 mL
1 cup	fresh blueberries	250 mL

- Line side of 8-inch (2 L) springform pan with waxed paper that extends 1 inch (2.5 cm) above rim. Line bottom and side of pan with Swiss roll slices.

- Stir gelatin into ½ cup (125 mL) cold water; set aside. In large heavy saucepan, heat milk just until bubbles form around edge of pan. Stir in vanilla.

- Meanwhile, in bowl, beat egg yolks well; gradually beat in sugar. Stir in hot milk; return to saucepan. Cook, stirring, over low heat for about 10 minutes or until thick enough to coat back of wooden spoon. Stir in gelatin until dissolved. Refrigerate for about 45 minutes or until partially set, whisking often.

- Whip cream; fold in sour cream. Fold into chilled egg mixture; gently fold in blueberries. (Mixture should be thick enough that blueberries don't sink to bottom; if necessary, refrigerate for up to 15 minutes longer.) Spoon into Swiss roll-lined pan; cover with plastic wrap and refrigerate for at least 8 hours or up to 24 hours. Remove side of pan and waxed paper; place cake on platter.

- GARNISH: Whip cream. Using pastry bag fitted with star tip, pipe meringue into rosettes over top and around base. Garnish with blueberries.

Makes 12 servings.
PER SERVING: about 435 calories, 7 g protein, 26 g fat, 46 g carbohydrate.

Golden Fruit Terrine

Edible flowers, such as pansies and roses, join the lushest summer orchard fruits in a crystal-clear jelly. This dessert is light, refreshing, and although it looks old-fashioned, it's very up-to-date in taste.

4 tsp	unflavored gelatin	20 mL
2 cups	white grape juice	500 mL
¼ cup	granulated sugar	50 mL
1 cup	sliced peeled peaches	250 mL
1 cup	sliced nectarines	250 mL
1 cup	quartered apricots	250 mL
¾ cup	orange segments	175 mL

- In small bowl, sprinkle gelatin over ¼ cup (50 mL) of the grape juice; let stand for 1 minute. Meanwhile, in saucepan, stir remaining grape juice with sugar over medium heat until dissolved. Stir in gelatin mixture until dissolved. Let cool to room temperature.

- Spray 8½ - x 4½ -inch (1.5 L) glass loaf pan with nonstick cooking spray. Arrange some of the peaches, nectarines, apricots and orange in decorative single layer in pan. Gently mix remaining fruit; spoon over top.

> **TIP:** Avoid aluminum pans because they can discolor the fruit. High-quality tinplate or steel-tin pans are fine as long as they are used exclusively for cold moulded desserts and have not been cleaned with abrasives.

- Set ½ cup (125 mL) of the grape juice mixture aside; pour remaining mixture over fruit. Place plastic wrap directly on surface; set another same-size loaf pan on top. Place one 7-oz (198 g) can in empty pan to weigh down terrine, making sure liquid does not overflow. Refrigerate for 1½ hours or until almost set.

- Remove can, pan and plastic wrap. Pour reserved grape juice mixture over terrine. Cover and refrigerate for at least 4 hours or until firm, or for up to 2 days.

- Just before serving, gently run knife around terrine. Invert onto serving platter; firmly shake downward to release from pan. To serve, cut into 1-inch (2.5 cm) thick slices with serrated knife.

Makes 8 servings.
PER SERVING: about 110 calories, 2 g protein, trace fat, 25 g carbohydrate.

VARIATION
SUMMER BERRY TERRINE: Substitute cranberry juice for white grape juice. Increase sugar to ⅓ cup (75 mL). Substitute 2 cups (500 mL) halved strawberries, 1 cup (250 mL) each raspberries and pitted cherries, ½ cup (125 mL) blueberries and ¼ cup (50 mL) red currants for the peaches, nectarines, apricots and orange.

Iris Raven's Red Fruit Salad

Refreshing and full of the best summer flavors, this chilled dessert has an unexpected crispness of luscious watermelon.

6	red plums	6
1 cup	bottled red fruit nectar	250 mL
	Rind of 1 orange, cut in strips	
¼ cup	granulated sugar	50 mL
1 cup	blackberries	250 mL
2 cups	raspberries	500 mL
1 cup	cubed seeded watermelon	250 mL

- Halve and pit plums; quarter if large. Place, cut side down, in single layer in shallow microwaveable dish; pierce skins in several places. Add fruit nectar and orange rind; sprinkle with sugar. Cover and microwave at Medium (50%) for 5 minutes or until tender-firm, rotating dish halfway through. Do not overcook.

- Add blackberries; cover and let stand until completely cool. Discard orange rind. Gently mix in raspberries and watermelon. Cover and refrigerate until chilled.

Makes 6 servings.
PER SERVING: about 135 calories, 1 g protein, 1 g fat, 33 g carbohydrate, high source fibre.

Strawberry Rhubarb Sorbet

Vibrant in color and taste, this beautiful sorbet seems so rich you could be fooled into thinking it's ice cream.

3 cups	chopped rhubarb (fresh or thawed)	750 mL
1 cup	granulated sugar	250 mL
2 cups	strawberries (fresh or thawed)	500 mL

- In saucepan, cook rhubarb with ¼ cup (50 mL) water over low heat for 10 minutes or until juices are released. Stir in sugar; cover and cook over medium heat for 5 minutes or until tender. Let cool. In food processor, purée rhubarb with strawberries until smooth.

- Pour into shallow metal pan; freeze for 3 to 4 hours or until almost firm. Break up into chunks and transfer to food processor; purée until smooth. Transfer to airtight container and freeze for 1 hour or until firm. (Alternatively, freeze in ice-cream maker according to manufacturer's instructions.) Store for up to 1 day.

Makes 8 servings.

PER SERVING: about 120 calories, 1 g protein, trace fat, 29 g carbohydrate.

Pink Grapefruit Sorbet

Sorbet is a divine example of the pleasures you can create in your own kitchen without an ice-cream maker.

4	large red grapefruit	4
¾ cup	granulated sugar	175 mL

- Grate rind from grapefruit to make 1 tbsp (15 mL). Squeeze juice and strain to make 3½ cups (875 mL). Set aside. In saucepan, stir together sugar, grapefruit rind and ¾ cup (175 mL) water until sugar dissolves. Bring to boil; cook for 5 minutes. Strain through sieve into bowl; let cool. Stir in grapefruit juice.

- Pour into shallow metal pan; freeze for 3 to 4 hours or until almost firm. Break up into chunks and transfer to food processor; purée until smooth. Transfer to airtight container and freeze for 1 hour or until firm. (Alternatively, freeze in ice-cream maker according to manufacturer's instructions.) Store for up to 1 day.

Makes 8 servings.

PER SERVING: about 115 calories, 1 g protein, trace fat, 29 g carbohydrate.

Strawberry Meringue Nests

Low-fat and impressive is how to describe these cocoa-dusted meringues filled with berries.

4	egg whites	4
¼ tsp	cream of tartar	1 mL
1 cup	granulated sugar	250 mL
1 tsp	unsweetened cocoa powder	5 mL
3 cups	hulled strawberries	750 mL

- Line baking sheet with parchment paper. Trace four 4-inch (10 cm) circles on paper; turn paper over and set aside.

- In bowl, beat egg whites with cream of tartar until soft peaks form; gradually beat in sugar, 2 tbsp (25 mL) at a time, until stiff glossy peaks form.

- Using large pastry bag fitted with small star tip, pipe meringue into border of rosettes around edge of each circle; pipe more rosettes inside to completely cover circle. Pipe second row on top of outer bottom row to form nest. Using small sieve, dust with cocoa.

- Bake in 275°F (140°C) oven for about 1 hour or until crisp on outside yet slightly soft inside. Turn off oven; let meringues stand in oven for 1 hour.

- In bowl and using potato masher, coarsely mash 2 cups (500 mL) of the strawberries. Slice remaining berries. Spoon crushed berries into nests; top with sliced berries.

Makes 4 servings.

PER SERVING: about 245 calories, 4 g protein, 1 g fat, 58 g carbohydrate.

Sour Cherry Fool

A fool is airy and simple, a pink cloud of fruit and the traditional freshly whipped cream. Here, pastry chef Donna Bartolini has replaced much of the whipped cream with low-fat drained yogurt.

1⅓ cups	low-fat plain yogurt	325 mL
2½ cups	pitted sour cherries	625 mL
⅓ cup	granulated sugar	75 mL
½ cup	whipping cream	125 mL

- Place yogurt in cheesecloth-lined sieve set over bowl; cover and refrigerate for at least 12 hours or up to 24 hours or until reduced to about ⅔ cup (150 mL). Discard liquid.

- In saucepan, stir sour cherries with sugar; let stand for 5 minutes. Bring to simmer over medium heat; cook for 6 to 10 minutes or until softened. Let cool to room temperature.

- Remove ¼ cup (50 mL) of the cherries; set aside. In food processor or blender, finely chop remaining cherries; transfer to bowl. Whisk in yogurt. Whip cream; fold into cherry mixture, leaving streaks. *(Dessert can be prepared to this point, covered and refrigerated for up to 1 day.)*

- Divide among 4 shallow dessert dishes; top with reserved cherries.

Makes 4 servings.
PER SERVING: about 250 calories, 5 g protein, 12 g fat, 33 g carbohydrate.

TIP: Fresh sour cherries can be hard to find. You can substitute 2 cups (500 mL) undrained frozen sour cherries or well-drained sour cherries in jars. If frozen cherries have been presweetened, reduce sugar to ¼ cup (50 mL).

Fresh Apricot Ice Milk

Food writer Iris Raven's roots are British and it shows in her creative touch with fruit desserts. The plus with this ice cream is that you don't need an ice-cream maker, but a food processor or blender is essential.

2 cups	chopped pitted apricots	500 mL
½ cup	granulated sugar	125 mL
1 cup	milk	250 mL
	Rind of 1 lemon, cut in strips	
2	egg yolks	2
1 tsp	vanilla	5 mL
½ tsp	butter	2 mL

- In shallow dish, mix apricots with half of the sugar; spread out in single layer, keeping pieces separate. Freeze until solid.

- Meanwhile, in small saucepan, heat milk and lemon rind just until bubbles form around edge of pan. Remove from heat; cover and let stand for 5 minutes. Discard lemon rind.

- In small bowl, whisk egg yolks with remaining sugar; whisk in hot milk. Return to pan; cook over medium-low heat, stirring constantly, for about 12 minutes or until thick enough to coat back of wooden spoon. Remove from heat; stir in vanilla and butter.

- Pour into shallow metal pan; freeze until firm. Break up into chunks; transfer to food processor. Add apricots; purée until smooth. Transfer to airtight container and freeze for at least 1 hour or until firm, or up to 3 days. (Alternatively, freeze in ice-cream maker according to manufacturer's instructions.)

Makes 6 servings.
PER SERVING: about 135 calories, 3 g protein, 3 g fat, 25 g carbohydrate.

TIP: To test whether custard is thick enough to coat back of spoon, stir custard, then draw your finger down back of spoon; the mixture should stay separated.

Microwave Lime Custard with Coconut

How about a dessert that tastes rich but isn't? This tangy, refreshing pudding has summery flavors but year-round appeal.

3 tbsp	granulated sugar	50 mL
1 tbsp	cornstarch	15 mL
⅔ cup	milk	150 mL
1	egg yolk, lightly beaten	1
½ tsp	lime rind	2 mL
2 tbsp	lime juice	25 mL
1 tsp	butter	5 mL
2 tbsp	shredded coconut	25 mL

- In 2-cup (500 mL) microwaveable measure, combine sugar and cornstarch; gradually whisk in milk until smooth. Microwave, uncovered, at High for 1½ to 2 minutes or until slightly thickened, whisking twice.

- Whisk one-third of the milk mixture into egg yolk. Whisking vigorously, return egg yolk mixture to measure; microwave at High for about 30 seconds or until thickened, whisking once. Stir in lime rind, lime juice and butter until butter is melted.

- Divide between 2 small serving dishes or ramekins. Place plastic wrap directly on surface; refrigerate for about 1 hour or until chilled.

- Meanwhile, spread coconut on paper towel-lined plate; microwave at High for 4 to 7 minutes or until lightly golden, stirring often. Sprinkle over custard.

Makes 2 servings.
PER SERVING: about 210 calories, 4 g protein, 8 g fat, 30 g carbohydrate.

Jellied Raspberry Quenchers

Making jellied fruit with raspberry concentrate and unflavored gelatin results in an authentic taste of summer. Serve in martini glasses, if you have them. They make this dessert look very elegant indeed.

⅔ cup	frozen raspberry cocktail concentrate, thawed	150 mL
1	pkg (7 g) unflavored gelatin	1
2 tbsp	granulated sugar	25 mL
1 tsp	lime juice	5 mL
1 cup	raspberries	250 mL
12	fresh mint leaves	12

- In saucepan, combine raspberry concentrate and 1⅓ cups (325 mL) water. Transfer ¼ cup (50 mL) to bowl; sprinkle gelatin over top. Let stand for 1 minute.

- Meanwhile, add sugar and lime juice to raspberry juice; cook, stirring, over medium heat until sugar is dissolved. Stir in gelatin mixture until dissolved. Let cool to room temperature.

- Divide raspberries among 4 stemmed glasses; pour raspberry mixture over top. Slide 3 mint leaves onto inside of each glass. Refrigerate for at least 6 hours or until firm, or for up to 2 days.

Makes 4 servings.
PER SERVING: about 125 calories, 2 g protein, trace fat, 30 g carbohydrate.

THE CONTRIBUTORS

For easy reference, we have included a listing of material by contributor — organized alphabetically, with page numbers.

PHOTOGRAPHY CREDITS

FRED BIRD: pages 21, 27, 41, 54, 57, 63,
65, 123, 126, 131, 133, 137, 141, 148,
157, 169, 177, 178.

DOUG BRADSHAW: back cover (left),
pages 9, 16, 18, 22, 25, 30, 33, 39, 48,
51, 61, 64, 93, 95, 96, 109, 116, 121,
143, 176, 181.

CHRISTOPHER CAMPBELL: back cover
(right), pages 67, 159, 172, 173.

CHRISTOPHER DEW: back cover
(bottom), back flap (top).

FRANK GRANT: page 112.

PAT LACROIX: pages 35, 44, 58, 66.

MICHAEL MAHOVLICH: pages 69, 75, 101,
102, 158.

MICHAEL WARING: pages 7 (top), 29, 37,
42, 113, 125, 128, 151, 164.

ROBERT WIGINGTON: cover, front flap
(top and bottom), pages 2, 5, 6, 7
(middle and bottom), 11, 13, 47, 53,
71, 73, 77, 81, 89, 91, 99, 115, 134,
145, 147, 155, 161, 163, 167.

DETAIL PHOTOGRAPHS
Design: Patty Watt
Photography: Ken Mulveney

INDEX